SOCIETY
AND THE YOUTHFUL OFFENDER

Publication Number 919

AMERICAN LECTURE SERIES

A Publication in

The BANNERSTONE DIVISION *of*

AMERICAN LECTURES IN BEHAVIORAL SCIENCE AND LAW

Edited by

RALPH SLOVENKO, B.E., LL.B., M.A., Ph.D.

Wayne State University
Law School
Detroit, Michigan

SOCIETY AND THE YOUTHFUL OFFENDER

By

CHARLES E. GOSHEN, M.D.

Professor of Engineering Management
Professor of Psychiatry
Vanderbilt University
Nashville, Tennessee

CHARLES C THOMAS • PUBLISHER
Springfield • *Illinois* • *U.S.A.*

Published and Distributed Throughout the World by

CHARLES C THOMAS · PUBLISHER

BANNERSTONE HOUSE

301-327 East Lawrence Avenue, Springfield, Illinois, U.S.A.

© *1974, by* CHARLES C THOMAS · PUBLISHER

ISBN 0-398-02934-2

Library of Congress Catalog Card Number: 73-9650

*With THOMAS BOOKS careful attention is given to all details of
manufacturing and design. It is the Publisher's desire to present books
that are satisfactory as to their physical qualities and artistic possibilities
and appropriate for their particular use. THOMAS BOOKS will be true
to those laws of quality that assure a good name and good will.*

Printed in the United States of America
Q-1

Library of Congress Cataloging in Publication Data

Goshen, Charles E.

    Society and the youthful offender.

    (American lecture series, publication no. 919.
A publication in the Bannerstone division of American lectures in behavioral science
and law.)

    1. Juvenile delinquency.
I. Title.
HV9069.G66   364.36   73-9650
ISBN 0-398-02934-2

INTRODUCTION

This book attempts to portray certain facets concerning the problem of delinquency which are not ordinarily emphasized in the literature on the subject. Much of the literature, and particularly that which attracts the most attention from the public and from legislatures, emphasizes the most dramatic aspects of the problem which, almost by definition, is least representative. As is generally the case with other issues of social behavior of people, the large majority of instances tend to be rather routine, undramatic examples which, therefore, attract little attention. The importance of redirecting attention to the more ordinary types of problems is far-reaching. In the past, law enforcement efforts, crime legislation, and prison systems have tended to be designed with the most vivid and most serious examples of delinquency in mind. The actual workload of the enforcement and prison system, on the other hand, has been made up mostly of rather different types of problems. As a result, the bulk of cases coming to the attention of police, courts and prisons are forced into a mold not designed for them.

Two major studies were performed as the basis for the report. One was a characterological investigation of youthful offenders in a state prison. The other was a research project in which the Durham decision was tested out in courts in the insanity defense of a group of defendants. The characterological attributes of delinquency constitute, in general, a major part of what could be regarded as the total assets and liabilities of an offender population. Knowledge of these, in turn, should be helpful in pointing the way toward both effective preventive and corrective programs. Heretofore, sociological rather than characterological features of offender populations have been the focus of attention. The former should be seen as an important, but incomplete part of the picture, while the two, together, represent something coming closer to a total picture.

The problem of crime and delinquency currently confronting American society is remarkable for the fact that there has risen notably few, if any, new approaches to the solution of the problem. Instead, forces at work are generally pointed in the direction of re-inforcing old solutions. Since, however, old solutions have never been shown to have been particularly effective, it seems timely that some new solutions be, at least, tried experimentally. A marked obstacle to the introduction of new efforts, in new directions, lies in the prevailing ignorance of delinquency on the part of social leaders. Almost no other subject demanding social action is colored by as much social distance between the problem population and the general population. Because of the remoteness of the one society from the other, those who pass and enforce laws against crime and delinquency use as their yardstick what they think would work for themselves, not what might work for the others. Truly effective preventive and corrective measures might well turn out to be those which the general, law-abiding society regards as painful and unattractive, even though effective in solving the problem. For instance, it already seems quite evident that standard forms of social punishment serve as deterrants to crime only in people who do not commit crimes.

Charles E. Goshen

CONTENTS

SOCIETY
AND THE YOUTHFUL OFFENDER

CHAPTER I

SOCIETY AND DELINQUENCY

THE CURRENT CRIME PROBLEM

FEW AMERICANS WOULD fail to conclude that a number one domestic issue in the United States today is the problem of crime. Popular polls attest to this prevailing view repeatedly, and politicians take advantage of it to the extent of making *law and order* a campaign issue (but not a dominant feature of their activities after being elected). There is much reason to suppose, however, that much of what seems to be an alarming increase and spread of criminal activities is merely new and more alarming news coverage. In any event, both the news media and the general public tend to hold distorted views, based largely on the fear that the news media has instilled in the public. Too often, for instance, the *respectable* middle-class citizen refers to a more peaceful past contrasting with a present violence which actually reflects only the difference between his own peaceful past life and the less peaceful signs he is now aware of in the community. In other words, in spite of the unchallenged assumption by many people that crime has been rapidly growing, as a problem, it might be, instead, that the most significant growth has been the awareness of what has already been there, but less noticed in the past.

In 1960 the United Nations sponsored a *Congress on The Prevention of Crime and the Treatment of Offenders* in London, and another one in 1964 in Stockholm. It was the conclusion of the conferees from many nations that crime was, indeed, on the increase—in all countries, and particularly among the youth of these countries. Furthermore, the increases noted appeared to coincide in degree and in timing with increases in the level of affluence of each country. Contrary to many common expectations, however, the increases were confined to crimes against property—that is, theft—and seemed to be associated with the simple increase in the number of things available to steal. In our own country, for instance, the increase in automobile ownership has correlated closely with an increase in car theft. Another noteworthy phenomenon which is rarely cited as relevant to the issue might be mentioned as well. As a given society changes from one which is primarily de-centralized and agrarian to one which is industrialized and more concentrated, there is a marked tendency to increase rather than decrease the regulations designed to govern all behaviors. Among other measures, these regulations take the form of an increasing number of laws which define criminal conduct. With increased numbers of laws to break, there is, therefore, increased incidence of lawbreaking. Car theft and all the traffic offenses which range from the serious ones of negligent manslaughter and drunk driving to the minor ones of parking violations were entirely unknown 75 years ago, yet represent a major share of police activity in the United States today. On the other hand, the crime of abandoning dead horses in city streets has largely disappeared.

A recent report which reflects the basis for much public fear, yet offers little evidence to make it sound scientifically convincing stated that, in the past year, one out of three central

---

SOCIAL MORALITY AND CRIME

It is probably true that our criminal codes do contain the *moral minimum* of our day and age. That is to say, those values which we hold most sacred and least dispensable are elevated by public opinion to the status of protection by the criminal law. Thus, many of the statutory enactments of our modern criminal codes merely redefine as criminal certain behavior which for many generations has been outlawed by the unwritten mores of our ancestors. These moral minima are found in the many criminal laws against the person such as murder, assault and rape; against the marriage institution, such as incest and bigamy; against public order and decency such as disturbing the peace and public immorality; against the state such as insurrection and treason. . . . Offenses of this type are condemned by all "respectable" and "right-thinking" citizens, and even abhorred by criminals themselves (especially when they are the victims). *Morals and the Criminal Law,* Richard C. Fuller, The Journal of Criminal Law, Criminology and Police Science, March-April, 1942.

---

city residents (in a certain large city) and one out of four suburban residents had been the victims of crime. Regardless of the merits of the various allegations, however, it is now clear that the public, in general, demands of government more effective action in curbing delinquent behavior. Consequently, measures will be taken which will be meant to solve the problems. There is no evidence, however, that any current proposal or program to do this is in any way different from what was done in the past, except to do more of the same (more police, more judges, more prisons). Since what was done in the past had little to commend it, therefore, it is unlikely that the desired results will be obtained unless some new ideas are introduced.

THE ENFORCEMENT AND CORRECTIONAL SYSTEM

Typically, the enforcement system becomes mobilized in the direction of a suspected offender when a citizen, usually the victim, makes a complaint to the police to the effect that a crime has been committed. For instance, the person who discovers that his automobile is missing, and presumed stolen, reports this to the police. There is very good reason to believe that only a tiny fraction of the actual crimes committed are reported, many of them not even being recognized as crimes (stolen property, for instance, might be thought to have been lost instead). In addition to those cases brought to police attention by a citizen's complaint, the police might originate certain actions against offenders when they are thought to be making a public nuisance or "disturbing the peace." The latter examples would often be public fighting or drunkenness, reckless driving or suspected drug traffic.

DISTRIBUTION OF DELINQUENCY

An unusual study reported in 1972 by the Center for Studies of Crime and Delinquency (National Institutes of Health) is to be noted. An entire "cohort" population was traced in respect to their contacts with law enforcement. All boys born in a given year in Philadelphia (10,000 boys born in 1945) were investigated through police and court records which would have included this group when they were between the ages of 10 and 18. It was found that 35 percent of the total had had at least one officially recorded contact with the police for suspected delinquent behavior. However, one half of all delinquent acts, and 70 percent of all robberies committed by the entire group were accounted for by 627 boys (6 percent). There was no evidence that any of the efforts made by the juvenile court system to rehabilitate these offenders had any effect.

The police exercise a very large amount of discretionary power which is not admittedly accorded them by law. For many reasons, ranging from lack of courage or corruption to commendable levels of understanding of human behavior, police will often let an offender go without bringing official charges against him. Innumerable family and barroom fights, for instance, are settled by the policeman's presence without the benefit of arrest, and minor offenses by juveniles are let off with a lecture, perhaps often with good effect. In addition, every jurisdiction is likely to place certain offenses or certain offenders off-limits as far as arrests are concerned because certain laws (morals laws) are not enforced.

When an arrest is made, the offender is generally brought before a police (magistrate's) court where formal charges are lodged against the offender. These charges specify which law has been violated, and the circumstances of the alleged offense. At this point, the offender might be placed in jail (city or county jail, or police station lock-up) to await further disposition, allowed to go home on bail after posting bond (to guarantee compliance with further procedures), or allowed to go home under his own or someone's else's responsibility without bond, to await further disposition. For minor offenses, such as traffic violations, the so-called fines are not the actual punishments levied for infraction of the law, but are forfeitures of bonds.

At some later date (as early as the next day, or weeks later) a preliminary hearing might be held. These hearings are usually before a justice of the peace or magistrate. In the case of minor crimes, and especially if the offender pleads guilty, the case might be settled at this stage by levying a fine. Otherwise, a trial date is set for either grand or petit jury and the offender is ordered to appear at that time. All of the very serious cases go before the grand jury before going to the petit jury, and the grand jury determines whether there is legitimate cause for a trial, and a reasonable amount of evidence of guilt. Grand jury proceedings tend, in most jurisdictions, to occur so infrequently that they have a major influence on the long drawn out process of settling the case. If the grand jury finds a *true bill,* the case is then scheduled for trial, which might occur a long time later. At this time, then, counsel for the defense enters into an adversary process against the prosecution, before a judge and a jury, for the purpose of determining guilt. Ordinarily, the jury has nothing to say about sentencing, for this is done by the judge, and in accordance with the criminal statutes which specify what punishments are to be meted out for each crime.

Theoretically, the offender's outcome does not depend upon whether he pleads innocent or guilty. Actually, the offender who is prepared to plead guilty is in a position to bargain with the prosecution for more favorable terms. One of the things the prosecution can do in the "plea bargaining" process is to reduce the charge to one which carries with it a lighter sentence in exchange for a guilty plea. Since these reduced charges then become the actual ones listed in crime statistics, they give a

---

THE NATION'S CRIME PROBLEM—NOTHING NEW

The President's Commission on Law Enforcement and Administration of Justice (Government Printing Office, 1967) reported on the incidence of crime and its trends, but pointed out, also, that there is nothing new about the problem or about the public outcry concerning it. A hundred years ago, for instance, contemporary accounts from San Francisco described the city as one "where no decent man was in safety to walk the street after dark; while at all hours, both night and day, his property was jeopardized by incendiarism and burglary." Teenage gangs gave rise to the practice, in New York City of police always walking "in pairs, never unarmed." A newspaper of the last century pointed out that in New York, "municipal law is a failure, we must soon fall back on the law of self preservation." During the Revolution, and before, "alarming" increases in robbery and violent crime were commonly reported. In 1910 an author declared that "crime, especially its more violent forms, and among the young, is increasing steadily and is threatening to bankrupt the Nation." The big city riots of the late 1960's had their precedents in the big anti-draft riots in New York in 1863, in the racial disturbances in Atlanta in 1907 and later (1919) in Chicago, Washington and East St. Louis, then still later in New York in 1935 and 1943. Between 1882 and 1930, 4,500 known lynchings took place. Almost no other examples will compare with the violence of the gangster wars of Chicago during Prohibition.

---

distorted picture of the spectrum of offenses committed, inasmuch as plea bargaining is a rather frequent occurrence.

For first offenses, and for minor offenses, particularly, the offender might be placed on probation instead of being sent to prison. During the period of time designated as probation time (usually equivalent to the length of time he would otherwise have been sentenced to prison), a number of restrictions can be placed on the offender by the court. He may be required to report to the court or probation officer at certain intervals, confine his travels to the limits of the court's jurisdiction, avoid associations with former friends, abide by a curfew, etc. If, during probation, the offender breaks one of these rules, he can be summarily apprehended and put in prison.

An offender sent to prison might become eligible for parole after serving a certain portion of his sentence. Usually at least one third of his sentence must have been served, and a satisfactory prison adjustment must have been demonstrated. Parole determinations are usually made by parole boards which are made up of people not connected with the administration of the prison. Parole, as is the case with probation, has a prescribed period of time during which the offender is discharged from prison, but subject to various rules of conduct enforced by parole officers.

Whether an offender is treated as a juvenile or as an adult is a matter of considerable importance. Typically, a juvenile is defined as someone under the age of 16 at the time of the offense, but in some systems, if the offense is a major one, it is treated as an adult crime. Juvenile cases are ideally investigated by probation departments of juvenile courts. Hopefully, these departments are staffed by social workers specially trained in this kind of work. The investigation is theoretically designed, not so much to establish guilt (as in the case of adult investigations by prosecuting attorneys), but to provide information which will assist in making the best possible disposition of the case. Juveniles might be held in custody during these investigations in "children's shelters," and unfortunately, sometimes in county jails along with adult offenders. When the needed information has been collected, an informal hearing is often held, rather than a formal one, before a juvenile court judge, and without a jury. Disposition of the case is supposedly decided without regard to the issue of punishment, but in accordance with the court's concepts of the best way to bring about a restoration of socially acceptable behavior in the juvenile. Thus, the juvenile might be placed on probation, under the supervision of a probation officer, or he (more often *he* than *she,* but including *she,* too) might be sent to a "reform school." Such institutions are called by various names, today, and almost none of them now have this as their official name. These institutions for delinquents offer more or less deprivation of liberty and more or less of something that might look like a private boarding school. Typically, juveniles are institutionalized for relatively long periods, but usually have indeterminate sentences.

Juvenile cases are, technically, not considered as criminal cases, and no criminal records are kept of them. Probably more often than not they are not represented by counsel and the usual *due process* rules do not apply. The rationale for this lack of application of *due process* is that the juvenile court proceedings do not, in fact, constitute criminal trials, and the disposition is not meant to be punitive. In a Supreme Court decision, *Kent v. United States* (1966), a case in which this author was involved for the defense, these assumptions were challenged. In this case, a client, age 16 was subjected to the informality (no counsel, etc.) of juvenile offenses during the investigation, during which time the prosecution built up its case, then the defendant was tried as an adult. The court ruled that a juvenile must be given the protection of due process when a serious crime is involved.

STAFFING THE SYSTEM: Perhaps the most glaring deficiency in the entire correctional system is the qualitatively and quantitatively inadequte staffing that prevails. In almost every phase of the system, from police to prison guard, prosecutors to defense attorneys, the American culture has accorded so little status and respect to the personnel working in the system that adequate numbers of candidates having adequate qualifications are rarely attracted to the field. Parole officers, for instance, could be extremely significant elements in the rehabilitation of offenders, but their numbers are pitifully small compared with their caseload, and in only a very few jurisdictions are they professionally trained. Criminal law, either at the prosecution

---

RELIABILITY OF CRIME REPORTS

The President's Commission on Enforcement and Administration of Justice (Government Printing Office, 1967) revealed some of the problems associated with assessing the nation's crime problem. For instance, the Uniform Crime Reporting system, recommended by the FBI, when it was adopted by the major cities showed an apparent large increase in reported offenses. These were paper increases rather than real ones because they were the result merely of changing the system of reporting used. As a result, between the years 1959 and 1964 when these changes took place, there was an apparent increase, in one year, of offenses reported because of the change in method used. For major cities, the paper increases in the year the change occurred were as follows: Kansas City + 202%; Buffalo + 95%; Cleveland + 63%; Chicago + 72%, Indianapolis + 47%; Nashville + 42%; Baltimore + 41%; Syracuse + 35%; Memphis + 31%; and Miami + 27%. Also, it was pointed out by the Commission that the FBI discontinued reports from New York City after 1949 because the data did not seem believable, including as it did, for instance, only one eighth the number of robberies as Chicago, but with more than double the population.

---

or defense level, holds little attraction to the bright young lawyer entering practice. There is a substantial role which phychiatry can play, also, in corrections, but the field of what is known as "forensic psychiatry" is attractive to very few in the profession. Judges are so poorly prepared for the complex decision-making they are required to engage in that many of them have fully admitted their limitations. The police suffer from the same problems, on top of which they are also being burdened with increasing responsibilities rising from the vast increase in poorly conceived laws. The system becomes, as a result, so inept that the rich and clever offenders have very little difficulty remaining free of its clutches, leaving only the poor and inept caught up in the meshes of corrections. Unfortunately, those which become the responsibility of corrections to rehabilitate are then the ones with the most limited resources—the ones most difficult to rehabilitate. As former Governor Maddox of Georgia said of his state's system; "Georgia could have a better prison system, if only we had a better class of citizen to put in them." The same could be said of the people who administer and operate the system.

A set of data which would probably prove to be a surprise to those citizens who have been impressed by the recent barrage of news which portraays "crime in the streets" as a rapidly growing menace is the trends in numbers of admissions to prisons. The following table (from Statistical Abstracts, 1971) shows the rate (numbers of prisoners per 100,000 population) of new admissions to state and federal prisons from 1950 to 1967.

Year	Federal	State	Total
1950	9.5	36.7	46.1
1955	9.3	38.5	47.9
1960	7.6	41.7	49.3
1965	6.6	38.8	45.4
1967	5.8	33.8	39.6

(RATE) ADMISSIONS TO PRISONS, 1950-67

The rate of admissions to federal prisons has steadily fallen to 60 percent of the 1950 level. The rate of admissions to state prisons (therefore the total) rose from 1950 to 1960, but has since fallen to about 75 percent of the highest level. Some critics of the present system might interpret this drop as an index of the alleged leniency being directed toward offenders, rather than as an index of the incidence of crime. The offenses known to the police did, indeed, climb during this period. The rate of reported offenses per 100,000 population rose from 1,123 in 1960 to 1,512 in 1965 and to 2,741 in 1970 (Statistical Abstracts, 1971). The rate of known homicides was reported as 12.4 in 1930, falling to 8.6 in 1940, then down to a low of 6.5 in 1955, but then rising to 10.4 in 1969 . . . but still lower than 1930. The number of arrests made in 1969 was 24 percent greater than in 1960, during which time the population had increased 13 percent—but more significantly, perhaps, during the same time, the total costs of operating the nation's criminal justice system rose 120 percent, with nearly a doubling of the police force. A point to be highlighted in these data is to the effect that changes in the number of arrests, or of known offenses might more often be determined by changes in the number of police than changes in the number of actual offenses.

The most conspicuous and demonstrable increase in recent years has been the increasing proportion of youthful offenders entering the criminal system. The total number of juvenile cases handled by courts went from 431,000 in 1955 to 1,560,000 in 1969. When traffic cases are subtracted from this list, the two numbers become reduced by 33 percent. In general, there was a 105 percent increase from 1960 to 1969 in the number of arrests of persons under the age of 18 but only a 10.5 percent increase in the number of arrests over the age of 18.

If the data presented here, or anywhere, concerning the incidence of crime, of arrests, of convictions, of the distribution of kinds of crime or related information seems confusing, incomplete or contradictory, it is no wonder. In spite of the fact that few types of human events have been so carefully recorded as have those concerning these issues, the data available leaves a great deal to be desired. For instance, each jurisdiction in the past has used its own classification system for categorizing crimes, each court has followed its own set of laws, customs and legal precedures not followed by others. Consequently, the great variety in quality of data has made it virtually impossible to collect them all into national totals. In recent years, the FBI has endeavored to induce the various jurisdictions to adopt its suggested uniform system of crime reporting. Over the years, a growing number of local and state governments have subscribed to this system, but even today the system is not in universal use. As a result, many of the national reports are markedly inaccurate, since they summarize different numbers of reporting jurisdictions each year, as new ones subscribe to the uniform reporting system. There even exists considerable uncertainly about how many jails and prisons there are in the nation, since the question revolves around the definition of terms. What is, or is not a jail or prison is not, in other words, a self-evident issue. For instance, large courts often have a number of locked and barred cells where defendants are held during trials. In some places these are called jails, and in other places they are not.

Estimates of the number of local jails (city or county) range from 15,000 to 41,000 depending upon how they are defined. There are often one or two locked room enclosures in some counties where subjects are held for short periods, but these often bear little resemblance to what one expects to see in a jail. Frequently there are *tanks,* which are simply large rooms with a number of cots in which a sizable number of the town drunks can be placed to "sleep it off." Whether these should be considered jails is, again, a matter of definition. Police stations often have *lock-ups* which might look like very secure and durable jails, but are only used to hold suspects for a few hours pending some disposition decision. Stockades in the military look and function much like other military barracks, yet serve a jail-like function. In counties which permit prisoners to work on roads and other jobs, dormitories are often provided for them, known as *workhouses* which might, or might not be considered as jails.

In 1970 a Jail Census conducted by the federal government listed only 4,037 local jails which were authorized to detain prisoners for more than 48 hours, and on March 15, 1970, there were 160,000 inmates in them. Typically, these are administered by the county sheriff, or in large cities by a jail superintendent. Almost universally, they are dirty, unsightly, poorly supervised and fit for nothing except confinement. Personnel who man these jails are typically those people in the community who would be otherwise unemployable, and often by *trustees,* that is, the prisoners themselves. In these local jails, about 50 percent of all inmates found there at any given time will be found to be there for alcoholic intoxication. The remainder will be those awaiting trial or court disposition, or those serving rather brief sentences (maximum 3 to 6 months). State prisons, on the other hand, are rather uniformly large, centralized and imposing institutions which look and are operated the way prisons are assumed to be, with a very major emphasis on security measures. There, prisoners are sent who have been tried in the state's courts, convicted of violation of state laws, and sentenced to relatively long terms (more than 3 to 6 months). There is still another type of state institution which is a kind of hybrid between a mental hospital and a prison, and called by various names, such as "hospital for the criminally insane." Again, depending on definition of terms, there are from 227 to 300 state prisons.

If there can be imagined a degree of elegance among prisons, the 31 federal prisons would probably deserve the highest award. Federal prisons, for instance, do get a *better class* of prisoner, since the so-called *middle-class crimes* are mostly federal offenses (income tax violations, counterfeiting, etc.) and relatively few federal offenses involve the very *common crimes.* Of the total of $7,340,000,000 spent in 1969 in the entire country's criminal system, the federal portion cost 8 percent of the total. Federal prisons tend to be operated in accordance with somewhat more advanced concepts of penology than other prisons, although they, too, place maximum emphasis on security provisions.

EFFICACY OF CURRENT LEGAL SANCTIONS

Massive evidence from many cultures and from many times, past and present, supports the conclusion that current criminal sanctions (arrest, trial, imprisonment, etc.) have little or no deterrent effect on those offenders who actually commit the majority of offenses. The very high incidence of *known* (and only a small, uncertain percentage of what takes place is known) recidivism points convincingly to this conclusion, for instance. It appears to be clear that criminal sanctions are invented, legislated and enforced in accordance with the set of values held by the Establishment of a society (hopefully, the nonoffenders). These values determine what is to be forbidden by law in accordance with what the Establishment considers valuable (private property, morality, human life), and the deterrent imposed is in accordance with what the Establishment would consider as punishment (public disgrace, loss of liberty). In the United States the Established tends to represent the views of business and professional people. Those offenders which most commonly attract the attention of police and courts, however, typically come from entirely different cultural backgrounds, with different values. This difference might, in fact, be the basis for the failure of the current system to control crime. There is some reason to believe that the sanctions applied do, indeed, have a deterrent effect on people who have similar values to the Establishment which promulgates them. Middle class women arrested for shop lifting are seldom found committing the same offenses again (or, at least, they are not caught the second time). In contrast, offenders from the more common lower socio-economic classes, not only are found repeating their delinquent behavior, but they tend to repeat the same kind, in a high proportion of instances.

The President's Commission on Law Enforcement and the Administration of Justice (1967) looked into these issues and came to the conclusions essentially as outlined above. They found, for instance, that of 1,186 cases of income tax fraud (middle-class crime) detected in 1963 to 64, only two persons were found later to have repeated the offense. Similarly, it was observed that the imposition of rather brief prison sentences on the group of corporate officers found guilty of price fixing in the Electrical Equipment case of 1960 seemed effective in correcting their illegal practices.

If any lesson is to be learned from these observations it might be that if punishment is designed to be used as a deterrent to crime, that the punishment selected should be the kind which has a motivating effect on the class of offender concerned. Thus, the typical, common offender who arises from the disadvantaged, disenfranchised portion of the population should have selected for his punishment one which clearly has a deterrent effect on him. That is, the kind of punishment which truly hurts him. The author surveyed a small portion of a prison population informally on this question, asking the members what they would consider to be an effective punishment for the other prisoners. Almost universally, they agreed that castration would have the desired effect. They reasoned that much of what the others (not necessarily themselves, however) did that was illegal was done out of an effort to assert their masculinity, and if that could be neutralized by castration, they would no longer have the temptation to commit crimes. They also agreed, though, that certain prisoners would be resistant to any punishment designed, and the quality thought to be present in them was simple stupidity—inability to learn from experience. Further, they tended to view the problem (of recidivism) as a kind of arrogance or sense of superiority which assumed an ability to get away with offenses without being caught. The outside observer, when he views the lack of education, sophistication, common sense or even of basic intelligence in the typical prisoner wonders how so much self-confidence could be expressed when prisoners make these assumptions.

CHAPTER II

PREVAILING CONCEPTS OF DELINQUENCY

THEORIES OF DELINQUENCY

THROUGHOUT THE NINETEENTH and the present century, theorists have postulated a variety of explanations for delinquent behavior. Few, if any, of these theories deserve to be distinguished by name or authorship, but most of them will conform to one or more of the following:

CRIME AS A CONGENITAL ABSENCE OF THE ABILITY TO REASON ETHICALLY: Harkening back to the case of the "Kallikak" family, as well as the concept of "moral insanity" of James Pritchard (1830's) and of the "criminal anthropology" of Cesare Lombroso (1870's), delinquent behavior has often been looked upon as an hereditary problem. Hereditary theories were used frequently in the last century to explain many aspects of human outcomes, and explaining delinquency in this fashion was in keeping with much of the prevailing thinking of the past. Although this kind of thinking, together with the Eugenics Movement, has largely died out in scientific circles, traces of it can still be found in folklore and in the legal system. The hereditary theory achieves a soul-satisfying purpose for the theorist in at least two major ways. In the first place, it tends to acknowledge an elitist view of mankind which places the theorist himself in the most elite position, with the delinquent in a congenitally inferior position. Secondly, the theory also absolves society of blame for its persistent failure to eradicate crime or rehabilitate the offender, thus justifying the current prison system of warehousing offenders. Fundamentally, the theory appeals to the kind of conventional mind that can conceive of no other way of viewing conventional behavior except that of being the *right* way to behave. Although many studies today will reveal to such people the sordid family and cultural background of the typical lower class offender which comes to the attention of the courts, these histories only serve to confirm the hereditary bias they already have formed.

An early challenge to the hereditary theory points out that since crime is necessarily defined, rather arbitrarily, by what particular laws are in effect at a given time, there is a substantial amount of learning involved in distinguishing between what is and what is not illegal. Since learning plays such an essential part, then the role of heredity would seem to be rather remote. The proponents of the theory then fall back on an ancient religious concept about the soul which implies an inherited repository of what might be called the *conscience.* The conscience makes one feel guilty when one has done wrong, and this serves as the guide in making discriminations between legal and illegal behaviors. Presumably, some people are born constitutionally bereft of this conscience, so do not have the capacity to feel guilty. This explanation was essentially the one promoted by Pritchard in his theory of "moral insanity." Later in the nineteenth century this concept became widely accepted in psychiatric circles but the term used was changed to "constitutionally inferior psychopathy." From this cumbersome diagnostic category has been derived the more simple and recent term: *psychopath,* while the constitutional implications have been largely abandoned.

CRIME AS A PROCESS OF YIELDING TO TEMPTATION: Another ancient set of assumptions, still residing extensively in the common folklore, is a basic concept of *good* and *bad* behavior. These assumptions view *bad* or immoral behavior as something inevitably offering pleasure (at least as a promise), while *good* or moral behavior is something which offers different rewards in the form of a sense of virtue. Thus, the former will always be presented to youth, particularly, in the form of difficult-to-resist temptation. The test of whether or not the temptation is resisted rests in something the folklore regards as "strength of character." Views of these kinds, most intensified in Calvinistic settings, regard delinquency as a kind of inevitable by-product of the assumption that virtue and strong character are never attained by all people. There is even a kind of tolerance in these views toward the wrongdoer, for they appreciate, at least, an understandable motive—that of pleasure-seeking—something which is

---

COMMENTS ON CRIME AND PUNISHMENT

In a speech by Edward B. Williams, chairman of the American Bar Association's committee on Crime Prevention and Control and published by the American Judicature Society in 1971, some notable comments were made by this leading exponent of the legal system. In answer to the hue and cry about how "soft on crime" the courts have become, he observed that "when a delinquent youth goes into the street to do his mischief, he doesn't go out because of (the decisions of) Miranda, or Mapp, or Escobedo, or Mallory, or Gideon. He doesn't give one fleeting moment of thought to his constitutional rights or procedural safeguards. He goes out there because he simply does not expect to get caught!"

He commented further to the effect that only 18 percent of all thefts of property ever get cleared on the police books, only 27 percent of instances of armed robbery get cleared and that 80 percent of all reported crimes (themselves only a small percentage of the ones actually committed) never result in an arrest. He places the fault on an inadequate police force and makes a plea for sharply upgrading the status and competence of police. It must be made an honorable and respected profession before any dramatic change can take place in enforcement. $80 billion is spent per year to defend our country from without, but only $500 million to defend it from within, and this is a disproportion of emphasis which is contrary to the real threats which face society. Swift administration of justice does not exist, and until it does, our system of legal deterrance has not truly been tested. The mere onslaught of paperwork associated with trials serves to delay justice and defeat their purpose. This can be streamlined. The antiquated methods of administration in effect, when modernized, could do a great deal toward bringing about the changes needed.

---

not without its own rewards. The proponents of these views, especially the militant ones, seem even to cherish the bad examples they can cite since they serve to dramatize the righteousness of the good examples (themselves). American style morality has, perhaps more than those of some other cultures, stressed the

negative side rather than the positive. That is to say, the pre-
scription for a conventional life is mostly a list of what the person
should not do. The American culture has eliminated some of
the ways in which other cultures have managed to make their
members appear superior to others. The mixing of many nation-
alities in the culture, for instance, has blurred the image of the
foreigner or stranger as an inferior person, and the absence of a
single national religion has eliminated another device in use in
some cultures for separating the *good* from the *bad*. What is left,
then, are the *good* and *bad* within the society which, to satisfy
the self-righteousness of the *good* members must be legally
labelled as such. Thus, the existence of both is necessary, and
no utopian ideas emerge to eradicate the *bad*.

CRIME AS AN EXPRESSION OF UNTAMED INSTINCTS: A pseudo-
scientific view of mankind has come to view civilization as a
recent, and incomplete, uprising of man from a state of savagery.
This view would see man as fundamentally, and instinctively,
brutal, selfish and exploitative. Among the conventional members of society, civilization has gradually replaced these instinc-
tive drives with more consideration for the rights of others.
However, not all people in the society have been imbued with
these civilizing restrictions on their native savage tendencies,
and these people become the offenders. The various Christian
religious doctrines have almost uniformly promised a way of
curbing anti-social instincts through salvation. The original concept of the penitentiary, for instance, was designed to do this,
largely through the agency of religion, and was literally meant to
be an institution where the wrongdoer would repent and be
saved. The first of the great prison reformers, John Howard
(1726-1790) had such a program in mind when he advocated
his reforms before the British Parliament. In more sophisticated
ways, Sigmund Freud also subscribed to similar fundamental
concepts. He, too, saw the uncurbed aggressive instincts of man
as pervasive, and kept in check only with great difficulty among
conventional members of society, but not under control by some
others. He was less optimistic than the religious people were
toward the prospects for bringing about a change in anti-social
behavior. There are American jails and prisons operating today

in which no semblance of rehabilitation programs are visible, yet none would deny a prisoner the opportunity to find the miracle of salvation through religion so often promised by the theologians.

CRIME AS A FAILURE TO LEARN CAUSE AND EFFECT RELATIONS BETWEEN BEHAVIOR AND ITS CONSEQUENCES: A rather straightforward psychological theory of more modern vintage views conventional behavior as the result of learning that good things result from good behavior. Similarly, bad, or delinquent, behavior would be expected to occur in those people who failed to learn this cause and effect relationship. More sophisticated versions of this view would stress the ways in which certain kinds of people never have the opportunity or experience of having had any personal influence over their own outcomes, but have, instead, been dependent for their outcomes on what others have done for or to them. These people, therefore, do not weigh the probable consequences to themselves of some immediate act, and thus end up committing acts which are illegal. Their intent is not necessarily one which is accompanied by a desire to perform anti-socially, but the anti-social quality of what they do is the unforeseen by-product of society's complex classification of behavior into *good* and *bad*. This theory does offer some logical route for rehabilitation through a graduated system of reward and punishment for behaviors of increasing degrees of complexity. To some extent, this is a mechanistic philosophy, since it is postulated on a conditioned-reflex concept of behavior which allows for nearly automatic reactions to stimuli instead of deliberate decision-making. The theory also does not allow for the possibility that a person might be aware of the unpleasant consequences of illegal actions, and abhor them, but regard himself as immune to the consequences because of his belief that he will not be caught. In any event, much of what passes for rehabilitation in prisons is founded on this simple psychology through the system of rewards and punishments awarded for the offender's success in learning and following the *rules*.

CRIME AS A MEANS OF EQUALIZING OPPORTUNITY IN LOWER CLASS CULTURES: A very modern sociological theory which interprets criminal behavior as a peculiar by-product of current cultural trends (and therefore not particularly applicable to the delinquency universally found in other cultures or other times), this theory places its stress on the common observation that most offenses which lead to arrests and convictions occur in the lower economic classes. As such, the theory would not be applicable to explanations for either middle class crime, or to the huge proportion of offenses which are not reported or never matched with an offender. The theory postulates that an outstanding attribute of current American cultural trends is a nearly universal belief that the material benefits of the affluent society are available to all people. In the face of such expectations, lower class, disadvantaged people when confronted with the inevitable but unpredicted obstacles to material success equalize matters through illegal actions. In other words, they correct the inequalities in the system of distributing wealth with short-cut, illegal, methods. This theory assumes an identity of aspirations in people, but a non-uniformity of capacity for achieving them through socially accepted means. In somewhat sophisticated ways, this portrays what simpler theories might have called, merely, greed. There is an implied, sociological, solution to the problem of delinquency in this theory. Presumably, if the opportunities available for attaining material comfort were truly equal, the foundations for crime would not exist. Such assumptions provide a philosophical justification for many of the recent "war on poverty" programs, and the failure of the latter to achieve their ends might well be indicative of a failure of the theory. The theory does not account for the fact that illegal methods are also prevalent among the economically comfortable as well as the economically disadvantaged except that the former more often find ways of avoiding being caught.

CRIME AS PREFERRED MODE OF BEHAVIOR IN CERTAIN GROUPS: Perhaps the most contrary to conventional ways of viewing delinquency, this theory sees some of the delinquency, at least, as a first option instead of as an accident or choice of last resort. It seems absolutely inconceivable to conventional middle class anglo-saxon morality that some of our own people would prefer the illegal to the legal route. Evidence for this heretical view, however, can be quite convincing in the study of many offenders (but not all). These people are likely to over-simplify the choices which are open to them as twofold: one route is the *respectable* one whereby the individual might get what he wants by virtue of hard work and much patience, waiting a long time for the expected rewards. The other route is the illegal one, chiefly through theft, which is much easier, quicker, and more certain of bringing the expected rewards. If, on top of this view of life, is superimposed a hearty dislike for hard work, or considerable impatience, then the second route might seem the better one. Such a process of reasoning can easily grant the risks involved in the delinquent mode, but weighs this risk against what might seem the greater risk of never getting what one works for with the conventional way, and finds the former risk not too great. If, still further, there is achieved a sense of power in one's ability to outwit the law, then the preferred delinquency might have even greater attractiveness. This kind of psychology is probably a fairly accurate characterization of the *con artist,* the swindler, types which are perhaps, more common than prison studies might suggest because they are not so easily brought to justice where they can be identified.

CRIME AS A DISTRIBUTION CURVE PHENOMENON: A detached, statistical view of man can easily reach the conclusion that for any definable characteristic, a normal distribution curve will illustrate the range of variations that characterize the members of a group. That is to say, for any given issue (such as delinquent versus non-delinquent behavior) the incidence of occurrence of a given characteristic in the total population will be reflected in the normal distribution curve, in which a few will show extremes at each end of the curve (both the superior and the inferior extreme), and the large majority will cluster around a mean. Theoretically, these findings suggest that the members of a population tend to conform to whatever the standards of the group are. However, in any population, a certain small percentage will deviate from that standard to a better-than-average level, and another small percentage to a lesser-than-average level. In the case at hand, the lesser-than-average would be the delinquents, and the better-than-average would be the moral leaders of the population.

More analytically, it can be postulated that any culture, in addition to developing a long list of forbidden or unacceptable behaviors, will also classify them in respect to how the prohibitions are enforced. Thus, a certain kind of forbidden behavior might be assumed to be so universally rejected by all members that no particular coercive effort needs to be made to enforce the prohibition. In our culture, for instance, it would appear to be unnecessary to make cannibalism illegal—not because it is acceptable, but because it can be assumed that no one would commit such an act. At the other extreme, another type of forbidden behavior is not coercively prohibited because it is either not serious enough to warrant making it illegal, or it seems uninforceable. Thus, the use of profanity might be an example of this sort. In between these extremes are the forbidden behaviors which are made illegal. Necessarily, however, these laws are deemed necessary because the forbidden acts *do* occur with some frequency, otherwise the law would not be needed. Consequently, the mere fact that certain behaviors are labelled as illegal means that society considers them, not only as unacceptable, but also as something which actually happens. This assumes, therefore, that delinquency is inevitable—that is, a product of the distribution curve phenomenon.

CRIME AS AN ACCIDENT OCCURING IN THE RISK-TAKING ACTS OF ADOLESCENCE: This theory is much more reflective of actual studies of people who are known offenders (but not the uncaught offenders) than the previous theories. The others, instead, are derived from implicit logic founded on (false?) generalizations made about people or the social system. Many of the offenders who actually end up in prison—the real *losers*—clearly provide evidence to make this theory credible. The adolescence of these offenders is often found to have been characterized by much experimental behavior which seems to be testing out the boundaries of how far they can go in taking various types of risks. Accidently, the experiments sometimes exceed the limits of what society considers acceptable, and delinquency is the result. This theory does not restrict this kind of experimentation to lower class adolescents, but claims that middle class youths have resources available to keep them free from painful consequences, such as imprisonment. Thus, a middle class youth is arrested for speeding or reckless driving in someone else's car, but is let off by paying a fine. The incident is described as a harmless lark and the car turns out to have been *borrowed*. The lower class youth, in the same circumstance finds that the car is classified as *stolen* and the adventure seems much less forgiveable, so he ends up in a criminal prosecution. More acutely, a youth breaks a certain kind of rule in school (truancy, smoking) and gets expelled, but with similar motives and methods breaks another rule (drunk driving) which leads to arrest. It seems an accident that both acts are forbidden but only one act was an illegal one and the other not. Another feature of this theory is an implicit assumption that delinquency almost inevitably starts during adolescence. Most offenders in courts and prisons do, indeed, demonstrate this kind of beginning. The type who do not launch their illegal careers until later life tend, instead, to be those who commit middle class crimes (embezzlement, etc.).

CRIME AS A SHORT-CUT TO SUCCESS: A rather typical socio-logical theory which is based on a fundamental, and questionable assumption, (namely: there exist universal laws of social be-havior). This theory begins with the proposition that the out-standing characteristic of the American culture is a strong orientation to success. This kind of thinking assumes all people, essentially, are caught up in a uni-directional achievement-ori-ented upward-striving. The criteria for success in this concept are standardized to the degree that any person who fails to achieve certain prescribed goals (high school diploma, college degree, material prosperity, home ownership, etc.) almost auto-matically becomes a "failure" and is so regarded by himself. Particularly those people who equate achievement with material affluence but find delays and impediments in the way of their acquiring it will be tempted to try the "short-cut" through de-linquent behavior. Thus, delinquency becomes merely an alter-nate means for achieving what all people seek, the motive in both cases being the avoidance of failure to meet standard suc-cess-oriented goals. By implication, the correctness of this theory would be supported if it could be shown that other cultures which do not subscribe to these uniquely American objectives would be relatively free of crime. Such, of course, is not the case. The evidence gained from actual offenders (known offenders) to support the theory is limited to the study of small numbers of articulate *con* artists who seek to identify themselves with mainstream society and to justify their delinquency in more or less socially accepted terms. The theory does not allow for sub-culture values which differ significantly from establishment values, nor does it explain the delinquency found in other cultures. The weakest assumption on which the theory is based is the one which seeks the expected universal law of social behavior. This assumption seems like a slavish search for scientific status through imitation of the assumptions of the physical sciences . . . namely the Newtonian assumptions of the existence of laws of matter and energy. Instead, it would behoove the social scientists to appreciate the human quality motivating some people which seek non-conforming roles in addition to those other people who seek the conforming role.

CRIME AS A REVENGE AGAINST A REPRESSIVE SOCIETY: This theory comes closer to being a justification for delinquency by the offender than it is to being a result of studying the typical offender. The theory portrays the offender as a rebel against society who chooses the forbidden type of behavior out of defiance toward what he regards as tyranny. Therefore, his delinquent behavior is an attempt to preserve his self-esteem by assertively resisting control. He would, therefore, be expected to be resentful of authority. Psychoanalytic theory would support the concept as a manifestation of the oedipal struggle to destroy the father (or the father image, namely, people in authority). Many of the adolescent problems seen in clinics do conform to this picture, and therefore there exists a substantial literature on these types of youths. They are not very common, but can be found, in prison populations. Because their rebellion is neurotic in the sense that it represents a misplaced aggression meant to be directed toward dominating parents, its delinquent character is not overwhelming anti-social, and there is a marked tendency for the adolescent to outgrow it as he gets older. It seems much more common among prison populations to find passive, dependent attitudes than aggressive and retaliative ones, and the wish to be accepted seems more frequent than the wish

CRIME IN AMERICA

The most natural and frequent question people ask about crime is "why?". They ask it about individual crimes and about crimes as a whole. In either case it is an almost impossible question to answer. Each single crime is a response to a specific situation by a person with an infinitely complicated psychological and emotional makeup who is subject to infinitely complicated external pressures. Crime as a whole is millions of such responses. To seek the *causes* of crime in human motivations alone is to risk losing one's way in the impenetrable thickets of the human psyche. Compulsive gambling was the cause of an embezzlement, one may say, or drug addiction the cause of a burglary or madness the cause of a homicide; but what caused the compulsion, the addiction, the madness? Why did they manifest themselves in those ways at those times?

The Challenge of Crime in a Free Society, Report of the President's Commission on Law Enforcement and Administration of Justice, Government Printing Office, Washington, 1967.

to get even. The typical rebel is, however, much more likely than other offenders to be highly articulate, more likely to find an audience for his views, and thus have a disproportionate influence on the attitudes of those who study offenders. The concept within the theory which portrays society as essentially repressive does not necessarily imply that all members are subject to the repression, but, rather, that certain classes of people are singled out for this treatment. The minority groups and the disadvantaged, particularly, are thought to be the objects of repressive forces, and this seems to be supported by the finding that it is mostly from these classes that most offenders are identified. As with many other theories, however, it does not offer an explanation for the anti-social behavior of other social classes, and for the many offenders which do not get caught.

CRIME AS A FAILURE IN ADAPTATION: A theory which stems from a view of social behavior based on concepts of "survival of the fittest," sees socially acceptable behavior as a success, and crime as a failure in adjustment. This theory is consonant with others mentioned which conceive of only one kind of objective as a motive for behavior, namely, achievement of standardized social success. It assumes that all people not only desire this outcome but are struggling to achieve it. Those with limited resources or with the largest obstacles become the ones prone to fail. The knowledge that a large percentage of offenders which end up in prison belong to the most disadvantaged, least educated, most discriminated against portions of the population supports this theory. However, it does not, as is the case with many other theories, explain the behavior of the many who commit illegal offenses but manage to outwit the efforts of law enforcement measures. It can account, only, for the *losers.* It also fails to acknowledge that many people not only avoid being caught, but truly make crime *pay* and achieve substantial degrees of success as measured by socially accepted criteria of measuring outcome (material success, public recognition, etc.), in spite of socially unacceptable methods of achieving it. The theory would be in sharp conflict with the one which portrays delinquency as a preferred mode of behavior, but would see it only as a choice of last resort. Clearly, the theory stems from little knowledge of actual offenders (both the caught and the uncaught), but is derived deductively from assumptions made about the social system. From the psychiatric point of view, the prime example of a failure at adaptation would be the kind of behavior described as psychotic and of the sort which leads to long periods of institutionalization. In these people, there is much more evidence than there is in the case of the delinquents, of a struggle to achieve socially acceptable levels of adaptation but which ends in failure. Both groups, the institutional psychotic and the institutionalized offender, tend to end up in a dependent or parasitic position vis à vis society. The social costs of one group are essentially the same as the social costs of the other, so to speak, yet one is considered more socially acceptable than the other.

CRIME AS A SUCCESSFUL MODE OF ADJUSTMENT: Apparently the opposite of the theory which sees crime as a failure, this one, nevertheless, is founded on very similar assumptions. In this case, the assumptions portray the world in which the delinquent has to make his adjustment as a different world than that facing other people. In the delinquent's special world, the delinquent route represents success in the sense that achievement of goals (material resources, etc.) is of sole importance, and the means used to reach them are pragmatically selected from those which seem to work best, crime representing one of the options. One quality which this theory possesses which gives it some credibility is the finding that among those offenders ending up in prison, such an outcome is not nearly as horrendous as it would seem to middle class, *respectable* people, and the world in which they enter after discharge does not stigmatize the prison record in the condemnatory way other portions of society do. Instead, getting caught and being imprisoned is likely to be regarded as *stupid* rather than immoral. The typical middle-class citizen supposedly faces few temptations to break laws and even fewer status rewards for anti-social prowess. Certain disadvantaged cultures, however, clearly face frequent temptations with many built-in rewards for yielding to them. However, the theory would be at a loss to explain the common observation that many members of the same families in which delinquents are found follow the non-delinquent route successfully, apparently in confrontation with the same kind of obstacles and opportunities.

CRIME AS ONE OF SEVERAL TYPES OF SOCIAL WITHDRAWAL: A highly credible theory which is applicable to certain types of *problem* groups, in which a certain portion of the delinquent population will be found is worth noting. This theory states that some people either never adopt or if they have adopted them, they later abandon all social norms and, essentially, retreat from society. Because they then appear to survive outside the boundaries of social behavior, they often appear to be problems to the rest of society. In order to retreat from society, these groups relinquish both the rewards and the demands of society. Thus, they seek no status, no acceptance and no material rewards from society except mere subsistence. Such people end up as hermits, as monks, as vagabonds, as eccentrics of various sorts (sometimes appearing to be psychotic), and as certain kinds of delinquents. A new and perhaps fashionable (in some circles) degree of respectability for these aberrant ways of surviving on the fringe or outside society is currently developing. Some of the *hippie* youth and *commune* cultures fit into this definition when they seek to survive on their own with minimal contact with established society. What makes them seem a problem to others is often the fact that they also tend to establish their own rules of behavior which can be markedly at variance with socially acceptable behavior (in re: sex, drugs, ownership of property, etc.). These new moves, if they prove to be durable and if they spread might well come to shake the established social system to the foundations, for the system does not admittedly allow for groups setting up their own rules. Nevertheless, there is an aristocratic precedent for this which deserves mention. Clearly, in the earlier days of development of our current English-then-American systems of social structure, the controlling aristocracy applied entirely different standards of conduct to the common man than it did to its own members. As late as the 19th century, American industrial aristocracy tended to hold itself immune to the rules meant to govern common man's behavior.

CRIME AS A MEANS TO AN UNRELATED END—DRUG ABUSE: Widely endorsed by courts, public officials and other spokesman and now increasingly accepted as fact by the public is the theory of drug-related crime. The importance of this relatively new theory is that it might well serve as a model for developing more comprehensive theories, although it now applies to only one segment of the delinquency problem. As is well-known, the theory states that delinquency starts indirectly in the adolescent with the taking of drugs. It goes on to explain that the youth typically becomes increasingly dependent on drugs to the point where his alleged *need* or *craving* for them, coupled with the rising cost due to increased dosage drives him to steal in order to get the money to "afford the habit." This theory is both simple enough to make it understandable to people and complicated enough to make it both intriguing and believable. It is no wonder, that it is widely accepted. The theory also serves other soul-satisfying ends. It places the blame for a great deal of crime on influences (those which lead people to take to drugs) that are not socially inspired. Further, it removes the blame from social institutions that are socially endorsed. In addition, it seems to explain why "good kids" can "go bad" without "really being bad."

It is rare today for this theory to be challenged, and its

widespread acceptance would certainly make the task a thankless one. The theory essentially suggests that the drug user steals in order to "support his habit" because he is driven to a point of desperation by the "craving for the drug." To those of us, however, who have worked therapeutically with drug abusers there is presented a more cogent question than the one answered by this explanation. The other question is this, "if the drug user is being driven to take desperate measures by dependence on drugs, why does it hardly ever happen that he becomes so desperate that he is willing to go to work, as other people do, to support his expensive tastes?" In spite of what many citizens believe, the work and profit from the petty theft which drug users engage in compete very unfavorably with the amount of work and profit which is involved in ordinary jobs. Nevertheless, the most difficult goal to reach with drug users (often more difficult than inducing them to give up drugs) is that of getting them to take and hold a job. In other words, it appears to the clinical investigator that much more significant than their willingness to steal is their unwillingness to work.

Obviously, a great many crimes are committed that are in no way connected with drug use. Also obviously, these offenders, too, have in mind some objective for which the offense is the means to an end. Those who steal, for instance, steal in order to gain the means for buying something they want. Rarely is this done for paying the costs of mere subsistance, but rather for the purpose of purchasing something expensive and luxurious. Not infrequently, it is for the purpose of "showing off," and this might take the form of stealing in order to acquire the means of buying an expensive car. Consistent with the drug-related-crime theory, it would follow from such examples that there also exist many cases of "automobile-induced-crime," or for other examples "women-induced-crime," or "trips-to-Europe-induced-crime." Common to all examples, however, is another phenomenon of more pervasive significance, and that is a resistance toward work as a means of gaining the wherewithal for paying the costs of one's expensive tastes.

The credibility for the "drug-induced-crime" theory is greatly strengthened by the wildly inflated prices which police reports attribute to drug costs on the black market. The police seize such a small amount of the drugs, and in such small batches, that they report their seizures as estimates of the retail price rather than the actual amount seized. Thus, instead of admitting that they seized only one ounce of 1 percent heroin, they report that they seized several thousand dollars worth. The truth would certainly make their efforts seem puny, but their claims of the dollar value of seizures make their efforts seem much more significant. Thus, the public is easily led to believe that the "cost of supporting a habit" can reach astronomical proportions. Actually, few drug users spend as much money on their drugs as the typical alcoholic spends on his alcohol. The drug abuser himself contributes to these illusions as he finds that exaggerated claims for the cost of his drugs often excites sympathy from others, once they have already accepted another dubious premise, namely, that the drug abuser is the unwilling victim of a terrible habit which has him under its control.

This theory is similar to some other theories in that it supports a prevailing set of assumptions about "laws of human behavior." These assumptions allow for only one way of thinking and behaving, and that is the way society prescribes. When exceptions to socially acceptable behavior are then disclosed these are most satisfactorily explained, without changing the assumptions, when it can be shown that the offenders are the victims of outside control which prevent them from behaving in the prescribed way. The assumptions can also be retained by showing that some of the exceptions occur in people who have not been exposed to the acceptable kind of influences. The assumptions are, however, disastrously violated by a proposition that suggests that one's mode of behavior might be determined by freely chosen options, one of the options being crime.

THE THEORIES IN GENERAL, SUMMARIZED: Nearly all theories proposed have a common denominator which is also common to many other types of theories of human behavior. The multiplicity of theories not only is indicative of the lack of acceptance of any one, but the inevitable dissatisfaction encountered toward each one. The common denominator lies in the tendency of the theory to assume universal motives for any given type of activity.

A striking example that shows how erroneous such an assumption is—that is, for each given behavior there must be a single and universal cause, or motive—can be found in a superficial study of voting behavior. During American presidential elections, there are typically 60 odd million people who choose between two candidates. The reasons each one votes for his particular choice are nearly as varied as are the number of people voting—but the number of choices is limited to only two. In human behavior in general, there almost invariably exist a limited number of options which people have to choose from, but a great variety of different motives which can determine the choice. The number of options available to meet any need or solve any given problem might be large, but the vast majority of people are aware of only a very limited number. The ones known to them are confined by their own narrow experience, by tradition, by the advice of others, or by the observation of what others are doing, and only in a highly selected and small portion of the population by novel means or by means which have been only used elsewhere. The reasons why people get married, for instance, could be found to number in the hundreds, or thousands, but the only choices available are "yes" or "no," or "now" or "later." The persons available to choose for marriage, furthermore, are limited to those few (one) who are agreeable to the idea. Similarly, the reasons, or motives, for delinquent behavior are very individualized and variable. The options of behavior known to the individual to express the motives are very few. Thus, a correct theory must be one which allows for the many variations possible, and besides, a given theory which might accurately explain a given delinquent act in a certain person does not necessarily explain other delinquent acts in the same person. The reason why people try something for the first time can be, and often is, different from the reasons followed on subsequent trials. In other words, it is absurdly naive to assume that for any given behavior there must exist only a single, standard motive. Furthermore, it would be equally fallacious to assume that the "causes" for "normal" or socially acceptable behavior are universal. Some people clearly follow the "respectable" route out of fear of the consequences of doing otherwise. Some follow it, simply, because

that was the first way they tried, and since it worked satisfactorily, it was continued. Some follow it because it is the only
way they know, some because they are imitating someone else,
etc. Almost precisely the same list can be made of reasons for
following the delinquent route.

Too many theories, practically all of the law enforcement
system, and the prison system most particularly are predicated
on a view of the offender which applies to only a tiny minority.
For instance, the operation of prisons, with their elaborate and
expensive security systems, assume an inmate population of
dangerous, hardened criminals who must, at all costs, be kept
under tight control. Magically, however, all these dangerous
qualities are supposed to vanish when the prisoner terminates
his sentence and returns to the community. Actually, however,
police competence is too limited to cope with this kind of offender. Instead, the incarcerated offenders are made up mostly of
those who are sufficiently amateurish and sufficiently unintelli-
gent that even the current degree of incompetence is equal to
the task of apprehending them. Thus, as time goes on, prison
populations get younger and younger as the ability of offenders
to outwit the legal system continues to progress while the competence of the system remains stationary.

An interesting phenomenon which is characteristic of public
attitudes at even high levels of sophistication is instructive. Not
infrequently, crimes are brought to the attention of the public
that are described as "senseless," meaning that no discernible,
understandable motive is disclosed. The Manson *family* murder
trials were examples. The conclusion reached concerning the
"senseless-ness" of the crimes implies that other crimes are, therefore, "sensible." A "sensible" robbery would be one, for instance,
in which "greed" was described as the motive, or a "sensible"
murder could be one which was done for profit, or out of revenge. The evident contradictions between these two types of
motives, not usually evident to the public, is not unlike a similar
set of contradictions concerning judgments in warfare. In the
latter case, there is widely accepted the notion that there exist
"inhuman" methods of killing people, meaning, by implication,
that other methods are "humane." Whether an enemy soldier

was killed by a rifle bullet ("humane") or by poison gas ("inhumane") would make little difference to the dead man or his family, of course. The assumptions underlying these contradictions is that all human acts should be carried out according to a set of rules, even when the acts are those committed as crimes or in the killing of people in war. As long as people follow these rules, then behavior is understandable, even though criminal. Otherwise, society must fall back on the conclusion that the person committing the acts was psychotic, the condition assumed to exist when behavior is not understandable. Such thinking, and such assumptions, accept as more or less inevitable the destructive behavior in question. Perhaps this very pessimism is what makes it inevitable.

Most of the attention directed by the public to the issues of delinquency focus on those acts which are regarded as most destructive and frightening to society-at-large—murder, rape, etc. Actually, of course, the vast majority of offenses are rather unalarming events. The crimes reported in 1969 from 4,627 jurisdictions to the FBI which led to arrests were as follows, for instance:

Arrests in 1969
(Excluding minor traffic offenses)

Offense Charged	Total Number
Drunkenness	1,405,000
Minor, non-traffic	1,097,000
Disorderly conduct	551,000
Larceny	482,000
Drunk driving	341,000
Other assaults	242,000
Burglary	240,000
Liquor laws	209,000
Narcotic offenses	193,000
Auto theft	117,000
Aggravated assault	101,000
Vagrancy	84,000
Carrying weapons	82,000
Embezzlement	67,000

Robbery	65,000
Gambling	63,000
Family offenses	49,000
Sex offenses	46,000
Prostitution	37,000
Stolen property	36,000
Forgery	33,000
Rape	13,000
Murder	10,000
Manslaughter	3,000
TOTAL	5,576,000

Fully 80 percent of these arrests were for offenses that were too minor to be considered as socially disruptive. A large percentage of them could be, and almost certainly will be, arbitrarily eliminated by the mere change in definition of drunkenness from *crime* to *illness*. When this happens, (and it has already got underway) the resulting sharp decline in arrest rates will undoubtedly be portrayed as evidence of success in the "war on crime," a success for which the FBI is most likely to claim credit.

Nearly all theories of delinquency assume that the anti-social behavior is a lifelong characteristic which first becomes manifest during adolescence. This bias is, again, one determined by the study of arrests and imprisonments, not a study of actual offenses. Adolescent offenders happen to get counted more readily than others simply because their inexperience makes them more likely to be caught. The opposite extreme, middle-class crime, is typically found occuring first late in life rather than during adolescence, but is less likely to lead to arrest. Although smaller in numbers of offenders, the amount of money involved in middle-class embezzlements exceeds the monetary value of other thefts by a very wide margin, for the latter rarely involve large sums while the former do. Typically, the middle-class offender shows a characteristic life-style differing little or not at all with other, law-abiding citizens, except for the crime in question, and, therefore, the delinquent behavior cannot easily be seen as a very provocative issue for study.

All theories commonly promoted to explain delinquent behavior make still another assumption which goes unchallenged. They assume that the difference between, for instance, taking a job in a department store in order to earn money with which to then purchase a new pair of shoes must necessarily have distinctly and qualitatively different causes than merely picking up a pair of shoes in a store and leaving without paying for them. On the other hand, this kind of thinking would not regard it worthy of drawing similar distinctions in causations to explain why one person elects to work as a department store clerk and another to play bingo in a church in the hope of winning a prize in the form of a new pair of shoes. The differences between the acceptable and the unacceptable methods of getting a new pair of shoes is determined by whether or not the individual follows a set of rules established by society, rules which can be arbitrarily changed in an instant by making bingo games either legal or illegal. Thus, the assumption in question makes a distinction in causation between following and not following someone's rules.

In spite of the challenge which can be offered to undermine any of the suggested theories, each one can be supported with some convincing evidence when certain offenders are studied. This peculiarity concerning these theories is equally applicable to other behavioral theories—namely, certain examples of behavior can almost always be found to prove any given theory. This phenomenon is merely a reflection of the human capacity to be inventive. That is, for every reason why some theorist can conclude people will do certain things, there can be found some people who do it for that reason. If it were possible, for instance, to invent an entirely new and novel motive for a given behavior, there could then be found someone who would use that motive.

Lastly, another fundamental assumption inherent in all theories presented concerning delinquency is the (naive) belief that solutions to social problems can be derived from such theorizing. In other words, a pseudo-scientific bias applies in these cases, in the assumption that solutions must be derived through abolition of causes. Thus, if causes of social problems can be attributed to *poverty*, then they can be solved by a welfare system which abolishes poverty. Instead, forty years of experience with an elaborate welfare system shows that social problems have been only subsidized, not solved. When human motivation is the issue of theorizing, allowances must be made for the elaborate use by humans of fantasy and inventiveness in addition to external forces and influences in the ways in which motives are manipulated by the individual. For example, for any given behavior which a person carries out repeatedly, he will have available, and will probably use, a number of different motives to do the same thing. The choice of what, when or where to eat a meal, for example, can be motivated by a dozen different motives which can, and do, change during the very process of making the choice or implementing it.

In conclusion, the point to be made concerning theories of delinquency is to the effect that no common theory bears up under scrutiny when its assumptions are challenged, and the value of pursuing theory is too little to deserve much attention. Instead, attention needs to be directed, in the case of delinquency, to the *phenomenology* of this kind of behavior—that is, the study of *what* it is rather than *why* it is. The *why* can be simply explained in the statement: "there are many different kinds of people, and they do what they do for many different reasons." Two people might have two different reasons for doing the same thing, or two people might have the same reason for doing two different things. Thus, for instance, stealing might be carried out because of either ordinary ambition to rise in the ladder of success or because of a desire to avenge oneself against an enemy. On the other hand, greed might be used by one person as a motive for stealing and by another as a motive for going to college.

CHAPTER III

A NEW APPROACH TO UNDERSTANDING DELINQUENCY

THE DECISIVE INFLUENCE OF THE FAMILY ENVIRONMENT ON DELINQUENCY

ALTHOUGH MASSIVE SOCIOLOGICAL evidence reported in the literature stresses the importance of delinquency having its major setting in a certain sub-culture of urban environments, too little attention has been paid to the much more discrete and decisive influence of the family environment. The kind of sub-culture, of course, to which the heaviest concentration of delinquency is atttributed is that found in the center or urban areas where are found the poorest, the minority groups, the largest families, and the most dilapadated conditions of housing, etc. In more recent years, there has come to be included the additional contributing feature of drug abuse. The police, the courts, the government anti-crime programs and large numbers of respected sociologists tend to subscribe to the view that delinquency is a by-product of this culture. Nevertheless, within these very sub-cultures there are found very large numbers, even a large majority, of people who do not, apparently, participate in delinquent behavior. Because the latter is so, therefore, the many proposals to "clean up the slums," or subsidize the poor or guarantee equal opportunities to the minority groups are not likely to have much impact on the problem of delinquency (although they might, indeed, contribute to the solution of other social problems). More attention than has been customary needs to be directed, specifically, at the kind of family environment which tends to breed delinquency. It does happen, however, that delinquent-prone family environments are most likely (but not exclusively) to be found heavily concentrated in urban ghettos. They are also found, but not as concentrated, in rural slums, and in middle class neighborhoods where similar family environments sometimes occur. In other words, preventive programs must be directed, to be successful, at the delinquent-prone family, wherever it might be found, instead of the delinquent-prone slum where many of these families are, indeed, found.

Robins,[1] for instance, in her remarkable follow-up study of delinquents, 30 years after being first identified in a child guidance clinic, found that the most enduring correlations found in those who continued a life of delinquent behavior, as compared with another group who did not, were certain family characteristics. Specifically, family disharmony, particularly when associated with an alcoholic or "sociopathic" father, was the commonest correlation. Typically, individualized (rather than group or statistical) studies of delinquent adolescents reveal a repetitive pattern occurring generation after generation. Severe family disharmony tends to be found, in the first place, where parents themselves had been, or are, delinquent; then their children tend, not only to repeat the same delinquent behavior them-

---

[1]L. N. Robins, *Deviant Children Grown Up* (Williams and Williams, New York, 1966).

THE BACKGROUND OF DELINQUENCY

In an article published in the American Journal of Psychiatry in March, 1972, entitled *Human Violence as Viewed from the Psychiatric Clinic*, Martin Roth, M.D. draws some conclusions. He has observed his clients tend to be concentrated in large centers of population and to be drawn from areas where social disorganization, poverty and physical dilapidation are marked. There is highly significant over-representation within underprivileged social classes and minority racial groups. The families tend to be larger and to be characterized by more conflict and disruption, more frequent changes of home, greater disharmony, a higher incidence of criminal conduct, more ill-defined standards and values, and worse discipline than the homes of neighboring non-delinquents. School achievement is poorer, truancy more common, the working career more often erratic and family rejection common. He points out the errors of other reports which claim that slum clearance projects would be effective in correcting the delinquency problem. Of all social factors at the heart of delinquency, none compare in significance with the decisive role of the family setting.

---

selves, but also to foster families of their own with similar disruptions and consequent delinquency in their children. It seems quite evident that the same kind of immaturity and impulsivity which makes for a disharmonious and irresponsible marriage also results in an excessive number of children, a poor work (education and economic) record, and a marked tendency to end up being a slum resident. It also happens, however, that other sets of factors can, and do, result in other kinds of families ending up as slum residents, and when family disharmony is not part of their home environment, delinquency is not nearly so common. Rarely are the true histories of these families (delinquent and otherwise) investigated or disclosed. A considerable degree of skill is needed to develop these histories, for the investigator will be invariably confronted by massive resistance and expert concealment strategies. Thus, too often, it is the neighborhood from which the delinquent comes rather than the home which becomes the focus of attention simply because the distinctive character of the neighborhood is so evident. It is no surprise, then, that courts, social workers and probation officers make the easy assumption that the problem of the youthful offender can be solved by removing him from his neighborhood environment and placing him in an institution. Seldom, if ever, is an effort made to correct the problem at home—the place to which the delinquent will likely return. On the other hand, the task of correcting these problems would be far from easy.

As Robins[2] and others have pointed out, delinquent individuals show a high incidence of a variety of behaviors which are indicative of low levels of successful adaptation to the standard culture, and other members of their family show a similar history of failures. Those kinds of behavior, other than the kind society classifies as delinquent, include: school drop-out, poor work records, dependency on welfare agencies, alcohol

---

[2]Ibid.

excesses, destructive gambling behavior, divorce and desertion, etc. It is interesting, however, to note that the females of the same families show similar histories, except that there is a strikingly lower incidence of illegal behavior recorded. That is to say, a very large proportion of delinquents labeled as such by courts and other agencies is in young males rather than females. Young females, only, can engage in that kind of behavior which yields illegitimate pregnancies, although it is only rarely that they then become labeled as delinquent. To one who has studied adolescent adjustment programs in guidance clinics (the author, for example), the degree and frequency of maladjustments found in males as compared with females does not seem strikingly different, except for the fact that the male more often manages to attract an official label of delinquency because some of his behavior is called illegal. Furthermore, in any given family, it is the rule rather than the exception for all members, or nearly all, to contribute their share of maladjusted activities . . . only one, however, might happen to have been adjudged delinquent.

The point of the above remarks, in summary, is as follows: Delinquent behavior in youth should not be regarded as being a

UNDETECTED DELINQUENCY

(Author's summary) An interview study of 180 adolescents aged 15-17, including both those with and without court records, disclosed that 93 percent of the total had committed a theft, including 92 percent of those with no records, 98 percent of those with one known offense, 96 percent of those with more than one offense and 86 percent of those in a correctional institution. Similar findings were disclosed for other minor offenses, but for the serious offenses, those adolescents with known records showed a much higher incidence of crimes. These findings suggest that traditional distinctions made between "delinquent" and "non-delinquent" adolescents must be misleading except insofar as they justify only conclusions about which get caught and which do not.

Court Records, Undetected Delinquency and Decision-Making, Maynard Erickson and Lamar Empey, Journal of Criminal Law, Criminology and Police Science, December, 1963.

distinctive class of behaviors which demand specific study or solutions in their own right. Instead, delinquent behavior, as it is labeled by courts and police, should be regarded and studied as indistinguishable in its cause and effects from a rather long list of other activities which all have in common the phenomenon of being failures in making a successful adjustment to conventional expectations. For instance, the delinquency associated with drug abuse could probably be abolished quickly and almost completely by merely providing free and legal drugs to those who use them, as is done under the British narcotics system. However, these measures alone would in no conceivable way solve the important social and life adjustment problems of these people. Furthermore, once it is widely recognized that the problem populations in which delinquency occurs present a much more extensive set of social problems than delinquency alone, it might well be that solutions to these problems will have to be regarded as unattainable. The tendency of problem families to raise problem children who, in turn, father (or mother) a new generation of problem children makes the prospects for solving the problem dismal indeed. The stringent measure of *compulsory* birth control, or *compulsory* sterilization, immediately suggests itself as a valid approach. Once the public becomes aware of these possibilities, pressures to enforce *compulsory* sterilization might well rise anew as they did fifty years ago. Foreseeing that possibility, efforts that might now be made to bring about extensive *voluntary* birth control in problem families might prove very profitable, and might make *compulsory* measures unnecessary.

CRITICAL MASS EFFECT

Another social phenomenon which is often alluded to, but not often cited as much as it might be for its probable importance, could properly be called the "critical mass effect." This effect would explain certain phenomena when a given concentration of certain social features in a population becomes contagious or self-perpetuating. If there is, indeed, a disproportionately high incidence of social problems in the populations of urban slums over and above the incidence of similar problems in similar kinds of people in rural areas, this explanation would seem to be a credible one. One might speculate as follows, for instance: in a given population of disadvantaged people in which social problems appear most likely to occur, one might identify three sub-divisions of that population. One sub-division (perhaps one-third) could be made up of individuals whose attitudes and resources more or less guarantee that they would not develop significant social problems in life. Another third might be made up of those whose background more or less certainly assures an outcome that will be characterized by problem behavior. The remaining third, on the other hand, might be sufficiently neutral or undecided or uninfluenced at a given time that they might subsequently lean in either direction. Then, whether this last group deviates in the direction of problem behavior or non-problem behavior might be determined by the environment in which they exist. When, for instance, the "critical mass effect" is not prominent—that is, where social problems are spread thinly through an area, then the prospects for ending up as delinquent might be slim. On the other hand, when the density of problem behavior is very high (e.g. urban slums), then delinquency might be the more likely outcome. Thus, two given populations having very similar demographic characteristics might differ markedly in the frequency of delinquent behavior, depending upon whether the "critical mass effect" is operative (high density of problems). In a high-delinquency environment, for instance, there can be expected a greater number of opportunities, greater degrees of pressures, and more acceptance for delinquent behavior. The "contagion" of delinquent behavior is tacitly accepted as fact by many judges and social agencies when they attribute delinquent acts to the influence of peer groups (e.g. to urban slum gangs) or the "associates" of the offender in question. Thus, solutions are often proposed that are designed to destroy these influences by separating members from their gangs, by neutralizing the influence of leaders, and particularly, by institutionalizing the offender (to separate him from the gang). Prohibiting the association of parolees with *known criminals* is a frequent condition of parole, in keeping with these concepts. Studies of youthful offenders indicates that an important factor resulting in delinquents and pre-delinquents associating with each other, then influencing each other, is one determined by default rather than by design. That is, it is evident that problem youths often

---

VICTIMS OF CRIME

One of the most neglected subjects in the study of crime is its victims, the persons, households, and businesses that bear the brunt of crime in the United States. Both the part the victim can play in the criminal act and the part he could have played in preventing it are often overlooked.

In the NORC survey of 10,000 households conducted by the Commission, there were five times as many whites as nonwhites, but the incidence of victimization among the nonwhites was 40 percent higher than among whites. The incidence of male victims was three times greater than for female. Victims among low income groups exceeded the rate for high income groups.

The Challenge of Crime in a Free Society, Report of the President's Commission on Law Enforcement and the Administration of Justice, Government Printing Office, 1967.

---

end up in associating with each other because they are excluded from other groups. Similarly, problem families become associated more closely with other problem families than with non-problem families by the process of exclusion by the latter rather than inclusion by the former. In other words, it might be quite accurate to state that problem people find each other, not by looking for each other, but as a result of the fact that they are ones left behind when other people pass them by—the others moving forward, the problem people remaining stationary in respect to maturation and development.

THE VICTIM'S ROLE IN DELINQUENCY

Another underrated factor in the occurrence of delinquent behavior is the role played by the victim of the crime. Some of the most obvious features which play a part in which the victim, so to speak, brings the crime upon himself to some extent include the following:

1. In certain crimes, and particularly many of those which are considered to be most serious by the public, the victim's role might often be almost equal in importance to the role of the offender himself. The police, for instance, tend to be most alert to the possibility that when the victim of rape brings charges of this crime against a given suspect, that the victim often has brought the act upon herself. The provocative sexual behavior of certain females sometimes assumes such a degree of importance in the alleged crime that the police frequently doubt that a crime did, indeed, take place. The prostitute might, for instance, be reacting with vengeance against a customer who failed to pay his fee; or, the more *innocent* girl might be making the charge to protect her own reputation. Even, in fact, when forcible assault did take place, the victim has often been found to have been a willing participant in seduction up to some point in the process. In another violent crime, namely murder, the victim has often been the aggressor who lost the battle. In other instances, the murder took place when the victim failed to follow the commands of an armed robber, thus sharing some of the responsibility for this crime. The frequency with which murder trials hinge on the offender claiming, or proving self-defense, indicates how often the role of the victim does, indeed, enter the picture.

2. The extremely prevalent series of offenses associated with theft of private property also frequently points the finger of responsibility to some degree toward the victim. In the first place, the victim might have failed to take ordinary precautions (e.g. leaving keys in car) to protect his property; thus, in essence, contributing to a considerable degree to the fact that he, and not someone else, became the victim. In more pervasive instances, the readiness on the part of the American public to expect insurance companies to pay for theft losses leads to failures to protect property, failure to report thefts to police, failure to cooperate in apprehending the offender, etc. Undoubtedly, all these influence some thieves to develop more confidence in their ability to get away with offenses than might otherwise

---

LOCATION OF CRIMES

One of the most fully documented facts about crime is that the common serious crimes that worry people most — murder, forcible rape, robbery, aggravated assault, and burglary — happen most often in the slums of large cities. Study after study in city after city in all regions of the country have traced the variations in the rates for these crimes. The results, with monotonous regularity, show that the offenses, the victims, and the offenders are found most frequently in the poorest, and most deteriorated and socially disorganized areas of cities.

The Challenge of Crime in a Free Society, Report of the President's Commission on Law Enforcement and Administration of Justice, Government Printing Office, 1967.

---

be the case. To this extent, therefore, the victim plays a part in bringing upon himself delinquent behavior.

3. In the commonest offenses of all, namely those associated with alcohol (except when damage to others is a part of the act), the victim and the offender is the same person—namely the drunk. Similarly, those drug offenses associated with both use or possession, and those connected with traffic in drugs are clearly dependent upon the victim for their continuation. Thus, many drug and alcohol offenses, as well as all *moral* offenses (prostitution, gambling, illegal abortion, pornography, etc.) are properly referred to as "victimless" crimes, meaning the victim and the offender are the same person.

4. It is sometimes observed that certain citizens or certain business establishments are victims of crime repeatedly, even though they, themselves, do not appear to be a part of the same world to which the offenders belong. The most obvious examples of this situation is the individual who possesses considerable property which then gets stolen more frequently than other people similarly endowed with wealth. Investigation of these people often reveals that they typically display their wealth in conspicuous ways in public, thus making themselves, perhaps unwittingly, logical targets for the thief to direct his attention

to. Homes, for instance, which are notably elegant, and in which live people who conspicuously travel, leaving their homes vacant, become targets. People who prominently display on their persons expensive jewelry, or people who gain publicity for their valuable possessions (e.g. gun and coin collections) also thereby make themselves targets.

5. The most obvious, and far and away the most common situation in which the victim provokes the crime is the case of the person who is an offender himself. Thieves not only are likely to be known to other thieves, but the latter are apt to know about the extent of each other's possessions and also likely to believe the victim cannot afford to report a theft of his property when it, too, was stolen property. Furthermore, people who typically engage in frequent acts of violence are the ones most apt to become associated with other similar people, and thereby make it likely to become victims of violence. The well publicized stories of what happens within the world of organized crime, for instance, where the members commit crimes on each other with apparently high degrees of frequency are other examples of the same order. The offender who ends up in prison typically becomes the victim of both the violent-prone behavior and the lack of respect for others peoples' private property that characterize the other prisoners.

In summary, the victim of crime is often the instigator, either directly or indirectly, to the extent that if he had behaved somewhat differently, the crime could have been avoided. It has been observed in another area of human activity that 80 percent of all accidents occur in 20 percent of the population, leaving only 20 percent of all accidents to be distributed among the remaining 80 percent of the population. Similarly, some equally small percentage (perhaps 20 percent) of the population tend to be the victims of an equally large percentage of crimes (perhaps 80 percent). Even more broadly, some 20 percent of the total population tend to account for some 80 percent of all social problems. Herein might lie a logical area for preventive programs. The prospects for educating victims in how to stop being victims might become more promising than educating offenders in how to stop being delinquent.

Not only do public policies direct inadequate attention to the role of the victim in causing crime, but even greater deficiencies exist in the attention paid to the victim as the injured party. Instead of viewing the victim as the object of concern, the prevailing view assumes that when a crime is committed, it is society that is damaged. This view of "crimes against society," or "against the state" arose first in early English law when all crimes worthy of public attention were assumed to be "crimes against the crown." Inasmuch as the crown did, indeed, own most of what was considered valuable enough to commit a crime against (especially property), this view had some validity. In the U.S., however, a similar rationale scarcely seems appropriate. It is most often the lives and property of private citizens and businesses which are the objects of wrongdoing, and the injury suffered is by individuals, not by the state. Nevertheless, the offender is expected to "pay his debt to society" via the punishment levied on him. Even when a monetary fine is imposed as

CHARACTERISTICS OF OFFENDERS

What is known today about offenders is confined almost wholly to those who have been arrested, tried and convicted . . . The offender at the end of the road (in person) is likely to be a member of the lowest social and economic groups in the country, poorly educated, and perhaps unemployed, unmarried, reared in a broken home and to have had a prior criminal record.

Offenders over 24 make up the great majority arrested for fraud, embezzlement, gambling, drunkeness, offenses against the family and vagrancy.

The 15 to 17 year old group is the highest for burglaries, larcenies and auto theft.

For crimes of violence the peak years are those from 18 to 20, followed closely by the 21 to 24 group.

One of the sharpest contrasts of all in the arrest statistics on offenders is that between males and females. Males are arrested nearly seven times as frequently as females . . . (However) the larceny arrest rate for women increased 81 percent from 1960 to 1966 in contrast to an increase of 4 percent for males.

The Challenge of Crime in a Free Society, The President's Commission on Law Enforcement and the Administration of Justice, Government Printing Office, 1967.

punishment, the money becomes the property of the government, not of the person who suffered injury from the crime. It might well be that this fundamental philosophical principle which specifies society, not victims, as suffering the injuries of crime needs correcting in order to make the basic changes needed in our criminal system. Perhaps, in other words, the beginning of change which might lead to sweeping improvements in peoples' respect for the legal system might be that of highlighting the significance of the injury to the victim. It is conceivable that another logical change would then be to assess punishments in terms of restitutions to the victim that are designed to compensate for the damages he sustained. Perhaps, then, the criminal system would become more understandable, and even acceptable, to many of those who now violate its covenants.

FORBIDDEN BEHAVIOR FROM THE ADOLESCENT'S VIEW

Perhaps no quality which characterizes the influences to which the typical adolescent is exposed stands out more vividly in his view than the long list of prohibitions which confront him. In other words, the adolescent is very likely to view the adult world into which he is in the process of becoming a participating member as one much more replete with "don'ts" than with "do's." Above all, these prohibitions appear confusing and contradictory.

On the other hand, the prevailing public mythology assumes the existence of clear-cut distinctions between acceptable and non-acceptable behaviors with minimal ambiguity. The myth also assumes that nearly all components of society—the family, the school, the legal system, the news media, etc.—are equally and uniformly acting as "agents of the culture." This assumption portrays all messages reaching youth as being uniformly in concert, directed toward the same ends (the common good) and calculated to teach him the distinctions between "right" and "wrong." Thus, the ancient, Anglo-Saxon legal test for "innocent by reason of insanity" has been the McNaughten Rule—the test of whether or not the offender knew *right* from *wrong* at the time of the crime. Only crazy people, in other words, are supposed to be unaware of the distinctions.

From the viewpoint of youth, in contrast to the prevailing

mythology, he is confronted with sets of judgements from many sources which evaluate behavior in ways that are quite contradictory to each other. The "agents of culture" with which he is in earliest and closest contact are his parents. More commonly than not, their translation of the message from conventional society on what constitutes acceptable and unacceptable behavior is far from accurate. Some of the forbidden behaviors listed by society, parents endorse as forbidden to others, but acceptable to themselves. Others they accept as forbidden by themselves and encourage others to think likewise. In addition, they add to the list another list of forbidden behaviors of their own. The school represents the second major source of outside influence in the young person's education; and it, ostensibly, preaches the conventional system of *right* and *wrong* behaviors. However, this tends to be a rather theoretical kind of pronouncement, for the school also has its own social system to control, and it establishes its own set of rules which it enforces with the means at its command. These rules differ markedly from those of conventional society, even prescribing when a person may and when he may not speak. Furthermore, the youth is exposed to the influences of his peer group which demand compliance with its standards of conduct in order to win acceptance. The typical youth quickly learns that at least two sets of standards prevail among his peers. One set is the conventional adult standard followed by some, and this practice is easily construed as being a slavish and unimaginative imitation. The other members of the peer group seem more imaginative and creative, giving rise to what appears to be a more unique set of standards which differ from those of adults, and therefore, might easily seem more fitting for the adolescent. Not until the young person ventures forth on his own to the outside world—outside of school and home—does he actually come in direct contact with the standards of conventional society face to face. This might not happen until he gets a license to drive a car or until he takes his first job. Until then, the message of society has been filtered through other agencies before reaching him, and necessarily appears to be somewhat distant, often less than credible, and frequently distorted.

To illustrate the multiplicity of messages which label behaviors as "good" or "bad," the following list of actions which
might be found in his repertoire are cited:

Act No. 1: Forbidden by society under threat of arrest and
imprisonment—
Condemned by certain members of peer group, admired
by others—
Successful completion of the act offers material reward—
Example—Store robbery

Act No. 2: Forbidden by school authorities under threat of
school punishment, ranging from simple admonition to
expulsion from school—
Ignored by most members of peer group, shared by
others—
Successful completion offers sense of triumph in outwitting
authority—
Example—Truancy

Act No. 3: Forbidden by parents under threat of parental
disapproval—
Generally endorsed by members of peer group—
Successful completion likely to yield a sense of indepen-
dence—
Example—Rebellion against father's authority

Act No. 4: Forbidden by members of peer group under
threat of rejection from group—
Generally encouraged by family, school, society—
Successful completion endears one to adults, estranges one
from peers—
Example—Reporting delinquency of a friend

Act No. 5: Forbidden by family, school and society with
uninforceable threats—
Endorsed by peer group who might share the experience—
Successful completion becomes sign of *growing up*—
Example—Sexual adventure

Act No. 6: Forbidden by conventional elements in society, sometimes by family, under threat of arrest—
Endorsed by peer group and some adult groups, both of which tend to hold themselves up as representatives of an *avant garde* viewpoint—
Successful completion yields sense of being *in* on important experiences—
> Example—Drug, alcohol adventures

Act No. 7: Officially forbidden by law under threat of arrest and legal punishment—
Widely practiced by all groups, not infrequently with boasting—
Successful completion leads to sense of triumph in ability to outwit law—
> Example—Automobile speeding

Act No. 8: Forbidden by law, threat of arrest, but only under special circumstances—
Encouraged by peers—
Successful completion results in defending one's honor—
> Example—Fighting

Act No. 9: Forbidden by published rules, under threat of personal injury—
Widely ignored by many people, silently followed by some—
Successful completion produces no consequences—
> Example—Violation of safety rules

Act No. 10: Forbidden by women under threat of simple disapproval—
Widely practical by males—
Successful completion yields sense of masculinity—
> Example—Use of profanity

In summary, the list of forbidden behaviors to which the adolescent is exposed includes only a tiny percentage which are also labeled as illegal, and only a small portion of these are actually seen by him as being enforced. Furthermore, each one offers the prospects of some sort of reward if successfully completed. Although the punishment resulting from the failure to get away with some of them is considerable, the punishment resulting from the others might seem very minor. Thus, it is no surprise to find many youths failing to mold their behavior according to the subtle distinctions which separate delinquent from non-delinquent acts. Clearly, those who do manage to make the appropriate distinctions without confusion are those who follow a particular conventional adult model, an asset which is often absent in the lives of some adolescents. Thus, a very large percentage of adolescents experiment with some delinquent behavior, even though a smaller percentage then make a career of it.

CHAPTER IV

THE STUDY OF YOUTHFUL OFFENDERS

OBJECTIVES OF THE STUDY

A STUDY WAS MADE, by the author, of a group of male youthful offenders (age 16-25) in a state prison specifically operated for this class of offenders. The major objectives of the study were as follows:

1. In contrast to the more common method of studying prison populations, this study did not assume that a prison population constitutes a single characterologically distinct group of people, but that more than one set of characterological categories would be found in a prison population, as is the case with any other large population of people. Therefore, a major objective was to identify and describe those groups which appeared to have their own distinctive characteristics.

2. In-depth rather than superficial investigations were conducted, again in contrast to the more common methods used of studying prison populations. Because in-depth studies require a vastly greater investment of time and skill than do the more superficial statistical studies, the number of offenders studied was necessarily limited. Futhermore, a limitation was placed on the sample of offenders studied because a moderate degree of voluntary cooperation was required, thus eliminating some members of the population which were not prepared to offer this level of cooperation. Approximately one sixth of a population of some 1,500 was thus studied over the period of a year. The purpose of concentrating on the more intensive, individualized approach was to uncover individual values and variations which would not ordinarily be disclosed by more standardized, detached methods.

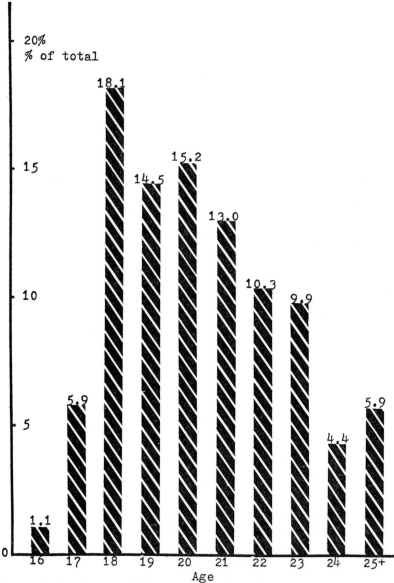

FIGURE 1. *Distribution of the prison population by present age.* Nearly 50 percent fell into the 19 to 21 age group. Most of the prisoners studied had already served a substantial portion of their sentences, so that the age at which they had been imprisoned averaged one-and-a-half years less. In other words, for this group, the age at risk is 17 to 20. This age range corresponds to the awkward period when this population is too old for school and too young and inexperienced to hold down a good job or enter military service.

3. The ultimate objective was not to *discover* the causes of delinquency, for this issue was considered to be a rather rhetorical one, but to uncover those characterological assets and liabilities possessed by a population of offenders which conceivably could point the way toward more workable preventive and corrective programs. In other words, rather than assuming that something could be found in the offender's life or personality which *caused* the delinquency, it was considered more likely that something might be found that was missing, something which a preventive or corrective program might be successful in replacing. In other words, many approaches to the problem of delinquency tend to take the form of looking for positive *causes* so that *cures* can be devised which eliminate these *causes*. This study, instead, began with the proposition that it was more likely to find delinquency happening by default rather than through the power of forces driving the individual from cause to effect. If delinquency often, or nearly always, happens by default—that is because something else does not happen—then prevention programs would logically be designed to supply something that was missing, thereby bringing about another course of events (acceptable social adjustment).

4. Another objective was to attempt to identify the kind of offenders that would be more likely to undergo successful rehabilitation under auspices other than institutionalization in a prison, assuming that prisons will continue to be used in the foreseeable future for punitive purposes, but, hopefully, for those more suited to that approach. Granted that prisons will continue to exist and be used, the important question becomes: what is the best way to use them? Or, how can the taxpayer get his money's worth out of supporting the prison system? Furthermore, it also seems hopeless to expect that society will, in the near future, abandon its demand that certain offenders be punished, regardless of what evidence accrues to prove that more problems are thereby created than are solved. Inroads into this punitive concept might ultimately be made, however, if certain offender populations can be identified which are shown to do better in response to some other set of measures. Already, sub-

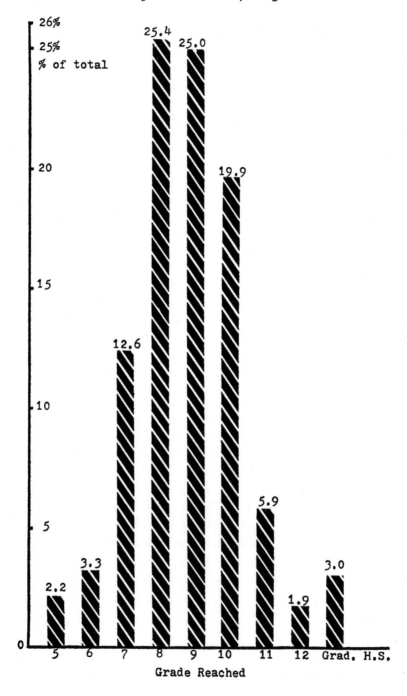

stantial numbers of wrongdoers are subjected to virtually non-punitive treatment (if imprisonment is used as the standard of punishment) by the use of suspended sentences, probation and fines. Very little credible evidence is at hand, however, to help courts and the enforcement system to identify those which most properly belong in prison.

5. Another issue which is rarely considered as relevant to the problem of delinquency is the question of what should correctly constitute short, medium and long sentences in prison. A fundamental philosophic principle implies that the "punishment must fit the crime." This principle assumes a gradation of short, medium and long sentences to fit minor, medium and serious crimes. According to what kind of logic, however, is it determined that a *long* sentence is 20 years, thus making 3 months a *short* sentence, and 3 years a *medium* sentence? It would seem to be equally logical (or illogical) to make one year a *long* sentence, one month a *medium* sentence and three days a *short* one.

In Denmark, for instance, the average prison sentence is less than six months (the U.S. average is about 33 months) and there is no reason to believe that the Danish compression of short, medium and long into much shorter time frames is any less justified. Therefore, another objective of the study was to seek clues to the effects which long sentences might have as a function of that portion of an offender's life spent in institutions compared with that portion spent outside. Few American citizens are likely to be aware of the fact, for instance, that many youthful offenders have spent up to 30 percent of their entire lifetimes in institutions, most often for a series of rather petty offenses. Clearly, then, institutional influences must have a decisive impact on those offenders' attitudes, skills and methods of coping with life. In contrast, a 45 year old accountant imprisoned 6 months for income tax fraud would have been subjected to drastically

---

FIGURE 2. *Distribution of prisoners according to highest grade reached in school.* 50 percent dropped out during the eighth or ninth grade. The legal age at which a student could quit school voluntarily was sixteen in the state, and a very large proportion of this population exercised this option.

different sets of influences, such that those imposed on him by the institutionalization would represent a relatively minor share.

6. Another hypothesis which provided directions for the study proposed the notion that there might exist a kind of symbiosis, or equilibrium between the enforcement system and that portion of the offender population which gets caught and convicted of crimes. The proposition suggests that the enforcement system tends to ignore certain portions of the offender population (not the least of which are those engaged in organized crime, as well as middle class crime) and concentrates its attention on another portion which is found to be more compatible with its capabilities.

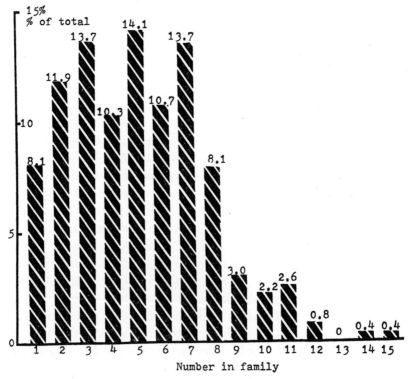

FIGURE 3. *Distribution of prisoners by number of children in family.* Over 50 percent of the families represented had five or more children. Even in the last century, it was noted that delinquent populations tended to come from large families.

Thus, the proposition implies that the incidence and frequency of arrests, convictions and imprisonments becomes a function of opposing influences in equilibrium with each other. Thus, as police competence in the detection and apprehension of offenders rises, the criminal skills of the offenders, too, rise. For instance, when police efforts shift from a low to a high level of competence in the enforcement of a particular kind of offense, then the offender population shifts from the amateur to the professional. In support of these conjectures, it appears evident that the number of arrests made per year varies directly with the number of police, not with the number of offenses. For that rather large population of youthful offenders which receive most of the attention from the enforcement system, it seems reasonable to assume that the vast majority of them are part-time, semi-amateur types of offenders. In this group, for every one which is removed from society through imprisonment, or removed from the world of delinquency by successful rehabilitation, there will be another one to take his place. In contrast, it might well be that total eradication of the professional, organized type of offenders from the offender population might have the opposite effect—that is, there might be no one to take their places. One phenomenon is quite evident in support of the hypothesis suggested. Those offenders who populate prisons tend to be, for the most part, those people who are well known to police and courts. It might be, ironically, suggested that police exercise a sort of quality control over crime, in that they tend to screen out of the delinquent world the bunglers, the inept, the unskilled, thus, leaving the field free for those better able to outwit the system.

7. Still another objective of the study was to identify concepts acquired by a prison population of what constitutes change in behavior. What the prisoner learns in prison, not about the difference between "right" and "wrong," as much as what is the difference between success and failure (in his terms) was a question to explore. This question arises as a corollary to the issue previously mentioned concerning the impact of institutionalization on the offender. Since among youthful offenders, a

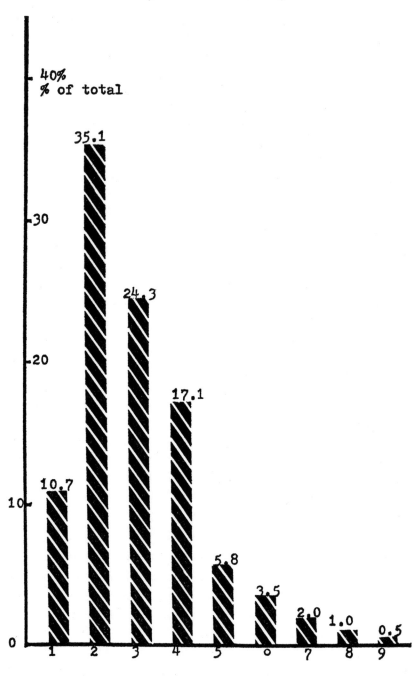

Number of Children in Family

large proportion of their total life experiences will have been those they had in institutions, these experiences should have a major bearing on what they have learned. Furthermore, these experiences have occurred, in the case of the youthful offender, at that time in his life when he is, more or less knowingly, learning how to become an adult. If the prison experience does nothing else, it, at least, provides the inmate with the time and incentive to make plans for his future when he gets out. These plans are almost certain to include what he has learned about how to avoid returning to prison. He might conclude, for instance, that the next time he is caught, he will seek the services of a particular attorney who has been recommended to him. Or, he might conclude that if he avoided going into partnerships with certain unreliable people, he could avoid being caught. Society, of course, expects that he will conclude that if he avoids illegal activities, he can stay free of prisons. Assuming, however, that he is very likely to plan to change something, the question arises as to what he, himself, expects to change. This should give a good index of the impact on him of prison.

8. Lastly, the study was curious about the previous influences on the offender of family versus the school. The role of family in the life of delinquent youth has sometimes been studied, and when it has, its decisive impact on the delinquent's mode of adjustment has usually been vividly highlighted. However, the other significant influence which children are exposed to, that of the school, has rarely been viewed as a competing factor of significance.

Hopefully, school influences are universally designed to be supportive of conventional social adjustment. Family influences are clearly not pointed in that direction as uniformly, therefore must often be competing with the influence of school. The fact that the offender population has failed to achieve a socially acceptable type of adjustment, therefore, indicates that the

FIGURE 4. *Distribution of a contemporary college student group by size of family.* A group of college students from the same general region as the prison reveals much smaller family sizes than the prison population did, with a mean in the neighborhood of 2.5 children per family.

school failed in this mission. Could this be because the school's influence is remarkably weaker than family influence, or could it be that schools do not, in fact, strive to exert a socially positive influence? The same question would be equally applicable in the study of types of maladjustment other than those classified as delinquency. The study of neurotic maladjustment, for instance, might properly raise the same questions.

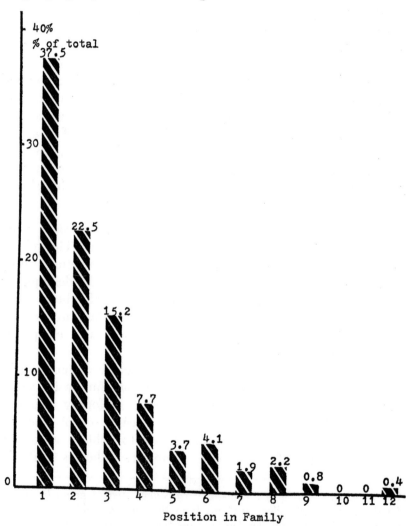

FIGURE 5. *Distribution of prisoners by position in family.* Almost 40 percent were first-born, which is higher than the statistical expectation.

METHODS OF THE STUDY

Interest in the study of youthful offenders was rather forcibly initiated by participation in a previous, not unrelated study. In the previous case, the study was conducted by a group in Washington, D.C., which set out to test the impact and effectiveness of the Durham decision in the District Courts (Federal). The Durham decision was a relatively new, and apparently progressive, modification of the old McNaughten Rule which provides nearly all courts of the U.S. and England with the basis for determining "innocent by reason of insanity."

The old rule relied on what has come to be considered as an overly simplistic concept of legal responsibility, based on the test of "whether or not the defendant knew right from wrong at the time of the crime." The newer Durham decision, written by Judge Bazelon in the Federal Court of Appeals (1954) concluded that the old rule was obsolete and that the defendent should be held "innocent by reason of insanity if he was suffering from a mental disease at the time of the crime, and if the crime was a product of that disease."

The research project which sought to explore this new decision undertook to either defend or serve as consultants in the defense of offenders in whom there appeared to be good reason to apply the new rule. Over a 3 to 4 year period, a substantial number of such cases was studied at length and this led to a rather unexpected commitment to explore the broader issues of youthful offenders in greater depth, and in other contexts. The report of the previous study has been published by Charles C Thomas • Publisher, under the title "Make Mad the Guilty," and written by Richard Arens, the principal attorney in the study. The author of the current study was involved as a psychiatric investigator and witness in the trials.

The facilities for studying a population of youthful offenders arose as a result of an opportunity to participate in a vocational rehabilitation project in a state institution for youthful offenders. The subjects studied were those members of the prison population who volunteered for vocational rehabilitation training prior to discharge. The training to be offered included that which could take place either in or out of the prison, and when the

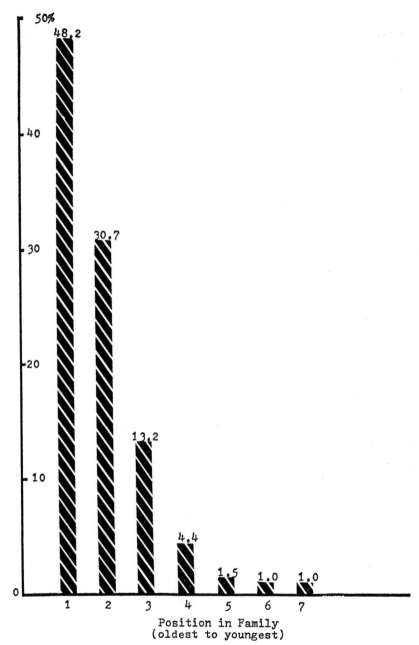

FIGURE 6. *Distribution of a group of college students by position in family.*
A state college serving the general geographic region of the prison, and

latter was the case, it was to begin when the subject either completed his sentence or started on parole. Thus, the subjects were those who, not only volunteered to cooperate, but who had already served a substantial portion of their sentence.

The prison housed some 1,500 inmates, of which one sixth volunteered for the program and were studied. Only prisoners between the ages of 16 and 25 were housed there, and only those with either relatively long (more than six months) sentences or previous records were selected for admission. Youthful offenders with short sentences or less serious records were more often kept in local jails. The prison was of relatively recent construction, in a rural setting, and midway in the study, an entirely new building complex was opened, which became the headquarters for the study. The state in which the prison was operated had about three million population, of which one third lived in one principal city. A disproportionately large share of the prisoners came from this metropolitan center. As might be expected, however, most of the state's poor and most of its black citizens came from this city. Large areas of the state outside the city contained populations with very high income levels and were predominantly white, but contributed very few members to the prison population.

A factor of more than passing interest, and one which was partially responsible for the launching of the project, should be noted. A major riot had taken place in the prison a few months before the project started. Upheavals throughout the state system resulted from the riot, including the resignation of the commissioner of corrections.

---

with comparable age groups was studied to compare the incidence of first-born. In this case 48 percent were found to be first in the family, but with smaller families, thus increasing the likelihood of being first born in the group. In both cases, however, the prison versus the college group, or the *losers* versus the *winners* of society more than the expected number of first born are represented. Many studies over the past hundred years have revealed that social successes are more likely to be first born than they are to be second, third, etc. in the family. One might speculate that the same finding among the prisoners might indicate a similar type of screening process at work in both groups, but the common denominator is hardly self-evident.

Those prisoners which volunteered for the vocational rehabilitation services were asked to submit their names, and
this list continued to be added to as new volunteers signed up
during the course of a year's time. Prison and probation records
were available for review. Intensive individual psychotherapeutic

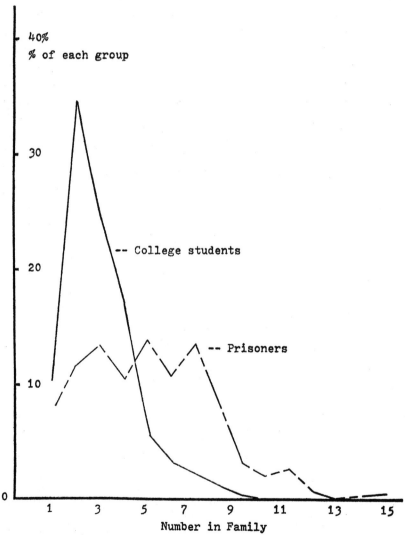

FIGURE 7. *Comparison of prisoners and college students by number of children in the family.*

interviews were conducted in a private office setting in the prison. The interviewing of each subject varied from a minimum of one hour each to a maximum of three hours. As the project progressed, it appeared increasingly evident that it was regarded by the prison population as one that was working in their interests and that the investigators were non-aligned with the prison administration. The level of cooperation was, accordingly, satisfactorily high and the degree of suspiciousness and distrust correspondingly low. Another reform measure was simultaneously put into effect in the prison, as a consequence of the riot mentioned. Prior to the riot, the use of parole in the prison was remarkably limited, but after the riot, parole was made much more available as one of the options open to prisoners.

Approximately double the number (from one third to two thirds of dischargees) of prisoners then left the prison on parole. Because both the new parole policy and the vocational rehabilitation project were simultaneously inaugurated, the prisoners tended to see the two as related. Thus, those prisoners more interested in, or more eligible for, parole were the ones most likely to volunteer. (A surprising number of prisoners disclaimed any interest in parole, apparently being more willing to serve a longer sentence rather than leave earlier under the conditions imposed by parole.)

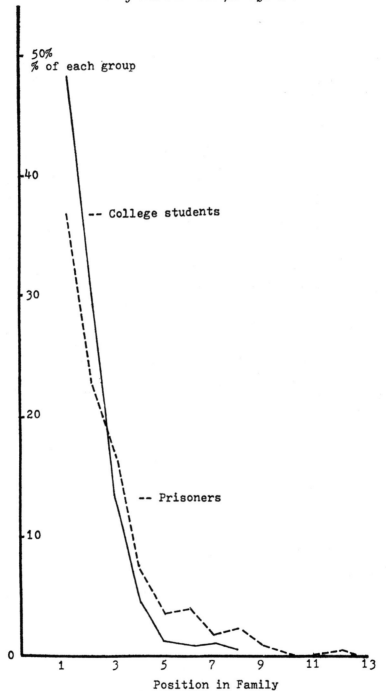

FIGURE 8. *Comparison of college students and prisoners by position in family.*

CHAPTER V

CHARACTEROLOGY OF YOUTHFUL OFFENDERS

OBSERVATIONS OF ATTITUDES AND RELEVANT BEHAVIOR

THE PROCESS OF investigating the offender population by means of psychotherapeutic interview techniques yielded substantial information of a nature which does not lend itself to statistical comparison. Nevertheless, in spite of the expected individualized differences in such qualitative phenomena as attitudes, a number of common denominators stood out which seem to be significant. The author has also surveyed other types of populations which provide a base for comparison. The objective in each study was to identify prevailing characterological features which appeared to be related to membership in a certain segment of the population. Certain general observations pertaining to all these population studies can be justified by the evidence. One such observation reaches the conclusion that when the criteria for membership in a given population is rigorous and rather highly selective, such that most people would not meet the qualifications for membership, then there tends to be a high degree of uniformity in characterological features. In other words, in the presence of a selective screening process, the common denominators or similarities are more striking than the differences among members. A simple example of this phenomenon is found in studying the characteristics of a general college population as opposed to an engineering school population. In the latter case, much more than the former, there will be found more striking similarities. The offender population in American society is, presumably, much more selective than the general population. As a result, a more narrow range of variation in characterology can be predicted. This study confirmed this pre-

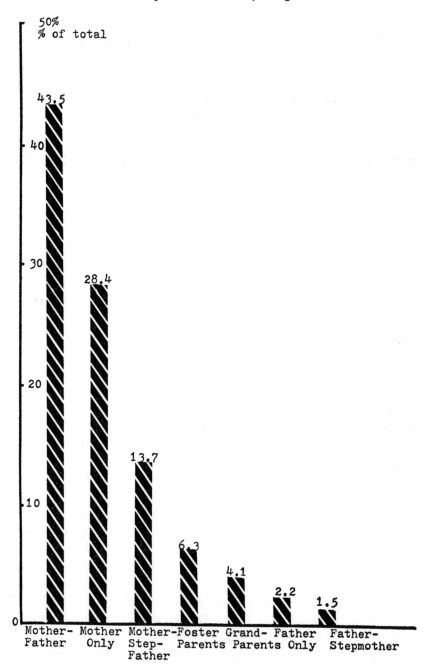

FIGURE 9. *Distribution of prisoners by type of family leadership.* In only 44 percent was there a father and mother present in the home during the

diction. Another general observation concludes that the more distinctive a given population is, characterologically, the smaller in size it is likely to be. Furthermore, sub-groups with differing characterological features tend to complement each other. Some of the observations made in this study are outlined below.

LANGUAGE SKILLS: A substantial majority of the offender population demonstrated a marked impoverishment of language ability. They tended to be rather uniformly unwilling and unable to communicate at length or in depth concerning any subject. Even those subjects, limited in number though they were, in which greatest interest was expressed could be rapidly exhausted in a few minutes. There appeared to be a general, apathetic lack of curiosity about acquiring more information about any subject. Their lack of experience in the use of language was made manifest by their awkwardness in putting together complete sentences, their very limited vocabularies and their frequent failure to understand other people. They often seemed to be sufficiently aware of their lack of language skill that they would rely on the help or leadership of others who were more adept in the use of words. Also, they often expressed a keen sense of isolation from people outside the prison (family, friends) because of their inability to write informative letters to them. In effect, much of the world which surrounded them all their lives had been shut off from them by the tenuousness of the communication links they had developed. Their language was overwhelmingly *present* centered rather than past or future oriented, as shown by the predominant use of the present tense. Their views of the world were apparently uncomplicated by any subtleties. This was manifest by an extravagantly limited use of adjectives and adverbs. Typically, they relied on the smallest possible number of descriptors to identify people, places, things, events, etc. People were "nice" or "mean," for instance, with often no other way of classifying them. Things were "big" or "little," but hardly ever "big as an elephant," or "little as a flea," or "bigger" than something else with which they might be familiar. When

---

five years preceding imprisonment. Most striking, and almost undoubtedly most significant, is the large percentage of familes with no fathers.

presented with choices of occupational objectives, they showed no sign of having a frame of reference for making comparisons. When both advantages and disadvantages of a given option were presented, these were merely confusing, and subjects tended to automatically reject any option which had a disadvantage. An outside investigator could easily come to the conclusion that the communication barriers were those imposed by the status differ-

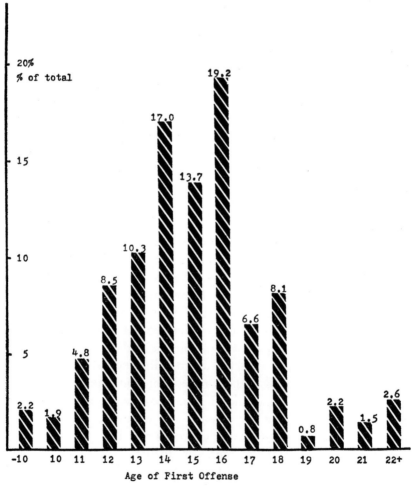

FIGURE 10. *Distribution of prisoners by age of first (known) offense.* 50 per cent of first offenses took place during the ages 14 to 16. A noticeable falling off of first offenses with later years is evident.

ences between himself and the prisoner. Observation of groups of them relating to each other, however, revealed that most of them participated very little in group conversations. Typically, conversations in groups were dominated by a very few verbal types while the others served as a passive, and apparently admiring, audience. The audience was evidently a necessary part of the communication taking place, since so much of it was designed to impress others. An investigator might, in view of these incidents, be inclined to conclude that the make-up of the delinquent gang was probably determined by these factors: a leader who expressed his executive ability by virtue of his communication skills, and a group of passive, uncommunicative followers who gravitated toward anyone who could act as a spokesman.

As might be expected, the fundamental vocabulary in use tended to be predominantly *street* language, in which rather precise and carefully used terms (chiefly nouns) were used to conform to the peer group's dictates. By the same token, and for similar reasons (survival), this primitive language was interspersed with highly technical legal terminology. Always, the correct and official term was used to describe the reasons for being arrested ("disorderly conduct," "second degree manslaughter," etc.). Also, the prison and its personnel were identified with official terminology ("this institution," "the officers," etc.); even though other, less endearing terms were in use among themselves. The most striking vocabulary deficiency was evident in looking for evidence of the impact of their school experiences. Rarely was any terminology evident which indicated that school had enriched the vocabularies of the subjects. Accents and syntax were usually suggestive of rural southern origins, coinciding with the family backgrounds of most of the subjects, both blacks and whites.

The vocabulary of responses to questions gave an index to the mode of thinking which appeared to prevail. A large percentage of all responses could be classified as those which the subject seemed to regard as either "good" versus "bad" (for him) or "safe" versus "unsafe." The frequency of this sort of response indicated that a vast majority of stimuli which the

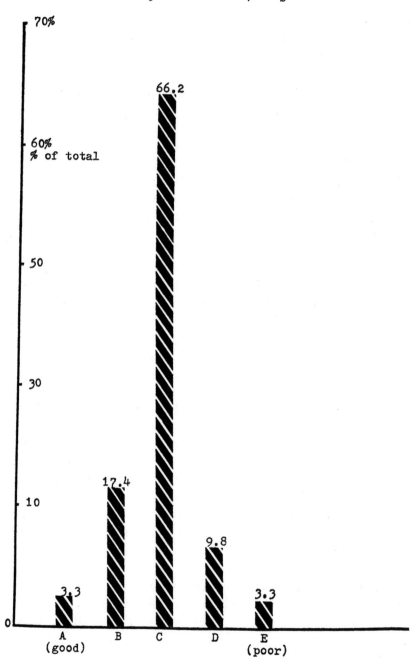

Adjustment Level

subject encountered were filtered and screened into these simple categories. A set of stimuli, on the other hand, which did not readily lend itself to this mode of categorization often produced confusion. Rarely did the subject seem to perceive himself as the repository of information which he might convey to someone else, and language did not appear to be used for such purposes to any considerable extent.

In contrast, however, to this predominant picture of the fundamentally uncommunicative offender, there stood out as conspicuous exceptions a much smaller group who were highly verbal, with richer vocabularies and aggressively spontaneous expressions. Unquestionably, many of the observations reported by the other studies which have been made have relied on these spokesmen for their information. Those studies which are spiced by the use of extensive *street* language are probably representative. Typically, these more verbal subjects present a very different case for themselves than do the more numerous but uncommunicative representatives of the delinquent culture. The latter almost certainly represent more of what might be termed the *army* of passive followers and the verbal representatives either the lone operators or leaders. A question of probably very profound importance, but debatable in the possible answers is "Do the followers typically seek and find their leaders?" or "Do

---

FIGURE 11. *The distribution of prisoners by level of adjustment to prison society.* An A level of adjustment was given when a prisoner had a minimum number of infractions of prison rules on his record, and was holding down a fairly significant job in the prison. At the other extreme, an E rating was used for prisoners with frequent infractions and no appreciable work record in prison. The middle level of C was given when few or minor infractions were on the prisoner's record, and routine, unskilled work records had been recorded. The remaining B and D ratings were given to prisoners who fell in between the middle and one of the extremes. As can be seen, two-thirds of prisoners fell into the middle group. This level of adjustment represented, more or less, the prison norm in the sense that it was a kind of compromise between doing enough to get by in the prison system, but with little evidence of efforts being made to do more than the minimum. In general, it would be safe to say that this level of conformity to society's expectations and of diligence in work would likely fall far short of the minimum needed to get by on the outside.

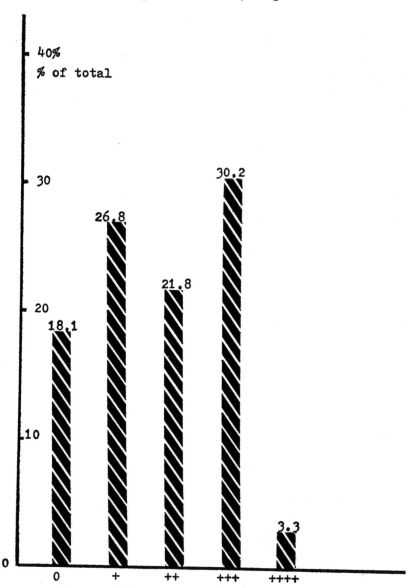

Level of Alcohol-Drug Abuse

FIGURE 12. *Distribution of prisoners by degree of alcohol-drug abuse. O* refers to those prisoners who were considered to be, essentially, abstainers from alcohol and drugs. "+" refers to the group which used alcohol only to a minor degree. "++" refers to the group which used alcohol regularly,

the leaders seek and find their followers?" Whichever of the two answers is more often the correct one would indicate where law enforcement effort, especially at the preventive level, should properly be directed. The findings of this study suggest that a program of great merit might be launched if new leaders were provided for the passive followers, then they could as easily be led into non-delinquent as into delinquent behavior. If the leaders were left without followers, then delinquency would assume much less alarming dimensions than now appears to be the case. A fundamental attribute of new leadership might well be the assumption of the spokesman's role in order to overcome the language barriers of the bulk of members of the delinquent culture.

ATTITUDES TOWARD SCHOOL AND EDUCATION: A remarkable degree of uniformity was evident in the bulk of young offenders in the matter of school experiences in particular, and toward education in general. Memories of past experiences with school were recalled as uniformly negative, but not with much hostility or vindictiveness. School experiences were usually portrayed as a *drag*, as dull, uninteresting and unexciting. In not one single case did a prisoner ever succeed in recalling a single teacher who had made a favorable impression on him. No teacher, in other words, had ever represented a model which the prisoner could cite as such.

Many of the prisoners were functionally illiterate, and only very rarely was any evidence of spontaneous reading found among them beyond comic books. Notable exceptions, of course, were found in a few who made extensive use of the prison

---

but not to such a degree that serious problems resulted. "+++" was the group of alcoholics in which drinking constituted a major problem, and was often associated with the activities leading to imprisonment. "++++" refers to the group in which drug abuse was a major and significant problem. When the youthful age of the offenders studied is taken in account, the large percentage of heavy drinkers and problem drinkers (++ and +++) is noteworthy, while the much smaller incidence of drug problems might be surprising to many. In spite of current folklore which assumes a high incidence of drug-related crime, the much more significant problem is alcohol-related social problems, including crime. Alcohol, for instance, is much more frequently related to violence than is drug abuse.

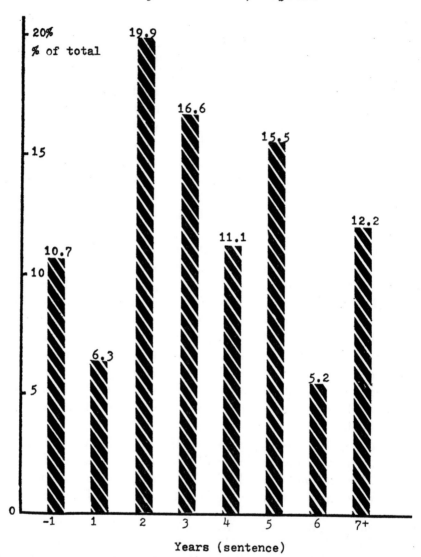

FIGURE 13. *Distribution of prisoners by length of present sentences.* A little more than half of the prisoners had been given sentences of three years or less, and a substantial number (12.2%) had sentences of seven years or more. The distribution of crimes by severity would not appear to be commensurate with the lengths of sentences. Instead, the long sentences for relatively minor crimes were related to frequency of previous arrests and convictions. The likelihood of an offender being arrested and convicted was clearly more closely related to his ineptness and lack of resourcefulness in

library. A rule of the prison, inexplicable to the prisoners, forbade the importation of books or magazines on the subject of the law, and the prohibited list also included the magazine "Playboy"—a factor calculated to stimulate interest in the relevant subjects. Schooling was offered on a voluntary basis to prisoners, but was made somewhat exclusive by the type of requirements imposed (good behavior). Largely because going to the prison school came to be regarded as a safer and easier task than the other activity options open (prison jobs or doing nothing), many of the prisoners elected to volunteer. Frequently, they surprised themselves by developing considerable respect for the teachers, even though they had not apparently had this kind of experience before in connection with school teachers. Actually, of all the prison personnel with whom the prisoners had contact (guards, the administration, chaplains, medical clinic personnel, etc.), the school teachers were held in higher esteem than any of the others. These experiences, and the discussions about them among the prisoners appeared to be often responsible for changing previously antagonistic or apathetic attitudes about school toward more positive attitudes. Not uncommonly, the prisoners would express regret over not having taken school more seriously in the past, and often promised to encourage younger siblings to avoid the mistake they made in regard to schooling. No other route out of the world of delinquency made as much sense to them as the one which education seemed to offer. Similarly, those who saw the correction of their educational deficiencies as a task beyond their capacity tended to view continued delinquency as inevitable.

It also seemed evident that when the prisoner himself had changed his attitude toward school from a negative to a positive one, his parents did, too. In retrospect, then, it appeared that the parents had previously given little encouragement to school achievement.

ATTITUDES TOWARD PROPERTY AND MONEY: In spite of the

---

coping with police and courts than to the severity of the crime. As one of the prisoners appropriately commented, "if you are stupid, you will not only get caught, but get caught often."

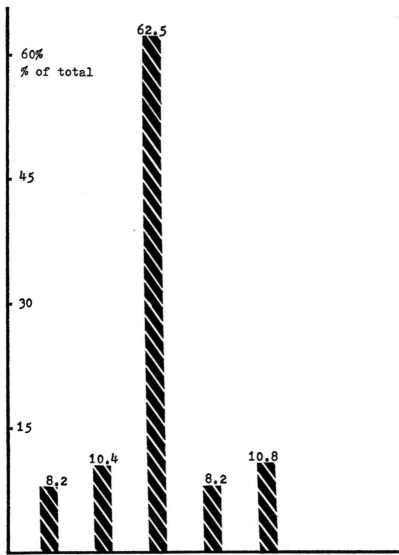

FIGURE 14. *Distribution of prisoners by type of crimes.* Crimes selected were only those for which the prisoners were currently serving sentences. Major crimes against property were considered to be those in which large scale burglaries and robberies took place, especially when armed. These included,

frequency with which the prisoners had been arrested for stealing, materialistic greed did not appear notably conspicuous. A standard question was posed to each subject, asking him to itemize what he would do with $1,000 if he were given that amount at the time of discharge from prison. There was generally expressed a distinct eagerness and sense of pleasure in facing this problem, initially creating the impression in the investigator that a long list of planned expenditures would be forthcoming. Almost invariably, however, once the prisoner had listed "clothes" as something he would buy with the money, he would run out of ideas. After much prodding, he might go farther and vaguely suggest he would like to give some money to his mother to make up for the periods when she had supported him, but this was usually done rather unconvincingly. In many instances, the prisoners had wives and children waiting for them outside, but never were these people mentioned as possible recipients of their generosity. Deeper investigation into their concepts of ownership of personal property revealed a fairly universal finding which would clearly distinguish this population from many others in the American culture. Except for occasional prized articles of clothing (e.g. an expensive pair of shoes), there was almost never a history of their having owned anything. Furthermore, their families typically never owned anything of lasting value (e.g. homes, cars, etc.). The fragmentary possessions found in their homes tended to be shared among many family members, with clothing being passed down from older to younger siblings, for instance. In essence, then, they had rarely had the experience

---

for instance, bank hold-ups and wholesale car theft operations. Major crimes against persons were those in which there occurred, or might have occurred, serious bodily injury. Minor theft included shoplifting, non-professional types of car theft and small-time robberies. Minor crimes against persons included street and barroom fighting. Crimes against self were alcohol and drug offenses.

The majority of cases, as shown, was made up of the minor thefts. This observation needs to be weighed against the distribution of prison sentences, the general lengths of which would seem to indicate a much greater proportion of major crimes. The typical prisoner was clearly one which fell in the group which had been convicted of a minor theft offense.

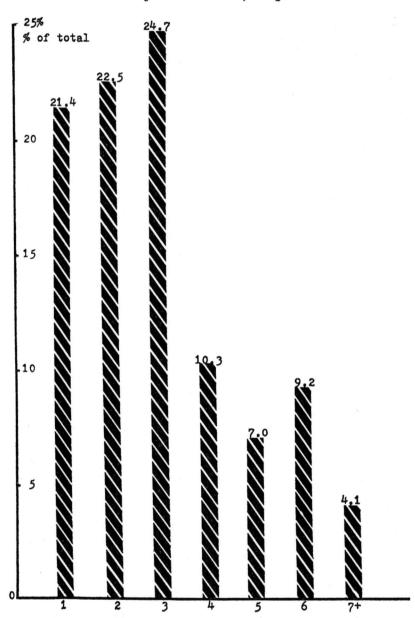

FIGURE 15. *Distribution of the prisoners according to the number of times institutionalized.* In only 21 percent of cases was the present prison sentence the first institutionalization. An equal percentage had five or more.

of protecting or treasuring something they owned themselves. Furthermore, their plans for the future did not include ownership of durable personal property. Pride of ownership must clearly play a major role in what might be called a corollary respect for the property rights of others, and in the absence of the former, it is no surprise that the latter would be missing also.

Money was generally seen as having value, and as being desirable to have in large amounts. However, it did not appear to represent much more to most of them than the status which possession of money might carry with it. It was not seen as a medium of exchange, which could be used to reach desired objectives other than making an impression on peers. Their concept of a large wage was repetitiously reported as $100 per week, apparently 100 being a much larger number to them than any weekly wage they had ever earned themselves.

In keeping with their general lack of experience in having known any pride of ownership, they seemed to see little damage done to those from whom they had stolen. It was inconceivable to them that a department store containing thousands of articles of merchandise would be in any way damaged by the shoplifting that had led to their arrest, for instance. Instead, the arrest seemed more to them like the enforcement of some arbitrary rule in a child's game. They, themselves, were often subjected to the thievery of their fellow-prisoners and would express great indignation over this.

In short, it would appear that the very large number of criminal offenses associated with the kind of theft for which these youthful offenders had been arrested (car stealing, shoplifting, etc.) was closely related to the differing set of values existing in the *haves* as opposed to the *have-nots*. In other words, the *have-nots* tend to steal from the *haves*. Furthermore, it would appear hopeless to expect people to acquire much respect for the property rights of others unless they, too, had property which they treasured and protected.

Summarizing, it can be tentatively concluded that there are likely to exist at least two links which most conventional members of society build up to cement their positions with society that are tenuous at best in large segments of the offender popu-

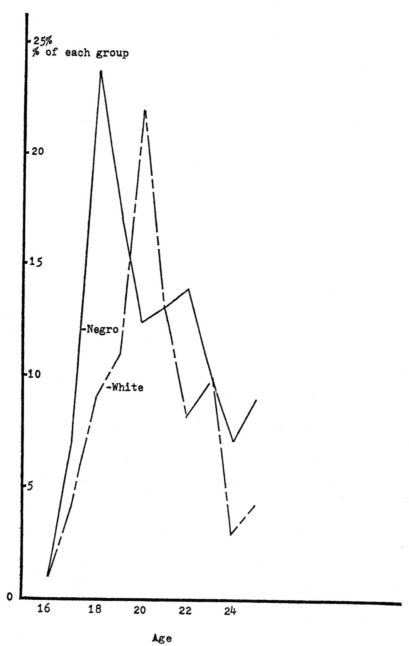

FIGURE 16. *Comparison of white and Negro prisoners by age.* The white population peaks one year later than the Negro group.

lation. These two links are: (a) the communication links with people in general and established institutions in particular which are dependent upon language proficiency, and (b) private property links which other segments of the population can view as part of their investment in the greater society, but which the offender group have few traces of. These deficits would clearly appear to constitute important mechanisms for the creation of the alienation, or "anomie," characteristic of problem groups in society.

ATTITUDES TOWARD FAMILY: Again, a remarkable degree of uniformity was evident in the prevailing attitudes existing toward the subjects' families. The same attitudes elicited by the investigator were also apparent in the discussions of prisoners among each other. Almost invariably, when the issue of family was raised, the prisoner responded with expressions of attitudes about the mother. The father was only very rarely introduced as a subject spontaneously. There was a general poverty of information extracted from the prisoners concerning the fathers. Often, it was not known where the father had emigrated from (usually the rural areas of the Carolinas or Georgia), or when; whether or not he had had military service, whether or not he had had siblings, or more than the barest of information concerning the father's jobs. The mother, not the father, was seen as the family provider, even in those cases when the father was regularly employed. In addition to the frequent instances in which a single father had been constantly present in the family, he was often found to have been relatively absent by virtue of being in the merchant marine, or working on traveling construction jobs. Most significant, perhaps, was the general absence of learned occupational information from the father. The father, whether present in the family or not, was not seen as a model. The mother, on the other hand, was clearly the focus of attention, and the only member of the family about which much was known. The mother was rarely seen as a punitive person, but more often as a passive, dependent one who tended to encourage dependency in the childern. Rarely were mothers pictured as having strongly disapproved of the arrests and imprisonments experienced by the subjects.

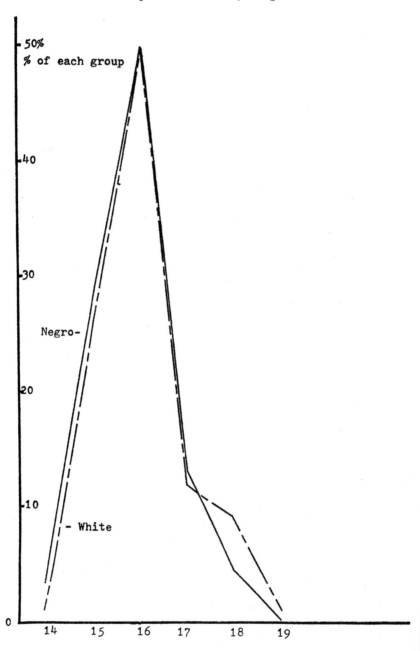

Age Drop Out of School

FIGURE 17. *Comparison of white and Negro prisoners by age of school dropout.* No difference is noted in the two groups.

The prison rules permitted each prisoner to submit a list of three persons with whom he was allowed to communicate and who were allowed to visit him. The mother was conspicuously present on the vast majority of these lists, and sometimes was the only one on the list. Plans for discharge almost invariably included going home to mother, and this occurred even when there was a wife and children in the picture. Wives would frequently have severed relations with the prisoner when he was arrested, but not mothers. The most dramatic promises for reform of delinquent behavior were those which centered on working to earn money to pay back the mother for the support she had previously provided.

In spite of the central importance of the mother in the subjects' thinking, there was scanty evidence of mothers' having exerted a positive influence in a leadership role in the family. They had rarely helped in school difficulties, rarely offered encouragement to occupational achievement and seldom participated in the subjects' defense at the time of arrest. By default rather than by positive evidence, the prisoners concluded that mother was the only person they could trust and who had some interest in them.

Siblings were usually numerous in prisoners' families. However, they, like the fathers, were pictured as nebulous characters about whom relatively little was known. It was not uncommon, for instance, for a prisoner to forget the names of some of his siblings, or their whereabouts. In some cases, older brothers appeared to have achieved a better adjustment, perhaps by having established a secure position in the military service. Nevertheless, these brothers seemed to have little or no positive influence on the subjects. Frequently, brothers had been partners in delinquency and might have been simultaneously arrested. It was more often than not the case that one or more siblings had also been institutionalized, as had the subjects being studied, a number of times.

ATTITUDES TOWARD JOBS, CAREERS, EMPLOYMENT: Perhaps the most striking feature related to job orientation in the subjects was an extraordinarily pervasive lack of information about the workaday world. There were extensive degrees of ignorance,

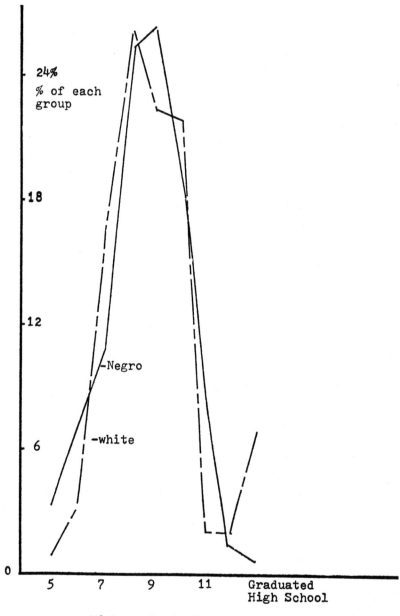

24%

% of each
group

18

12

—Negro

—white

6

0

5   7   9   11   Graduated
                             High School

Highest Grade Reached

FIGURE 18. *Comparison of whites and Negroes by highest grade in school reached.* The two distribution curves are remarkable for their similarity, the only difference of note being that the the only high school graduates

for example, concerning such work-related information as: social security, union membership, unemployment compensation, overtime, etc. Standard and traditional occupations were rarely known beyond their titles: steam-fitter, welder, rigger, carpenter, printer, etc. When the subjects' actual contacts with occupational categories were explored, it almost was never found that a person well known to them had held a highly-esteemed job. They had had contacts, however, with policemen, school teachers, landlords, and retail merchants, and had had occasion to see them performing their jobs. In almost no instance, however, was the view they obtained one which prompted them to take an interest in that occupation.

The framework around which this study of youthful offenders was conducted centered on a vocational rehabilitation project, in which the prisoners were investigated in respect to their interests and potential for profiting from vocational training. In this program, a number of discrete job training opportunities was available to choose from, and which was then to be matched with the prisoners' capacities. The project staff predicted that one of the options likely to prove popular was heavy equipment operator training (bulldozer, earth moving equipment, etc.). The training would include an out-of-state placement for a number of months, in an occupation which enjoyed a reputation for being relatively tolerant of candidates with prison records. However, this did not prove to be popular, and many of the prisoners who elected the option quit the training before completion. The prospects for being away from home, and away from the environment in which they had had enormous troubles—where they had established very unfavorable reputations—had little appeal. They tended to gravitate, in other words, back to the same environment where the local police had them already on the list of suspects for all future offenses, where opportunities had already proven scarce, and where few re-

---

were found among whites (6%) The critical period of schooling in the lives of both groups should be considered as the one or two years preceding the ninth grade, that is, in junior high school. By the time this group reached high school age they had already dropped out, or were in the process of doing so.

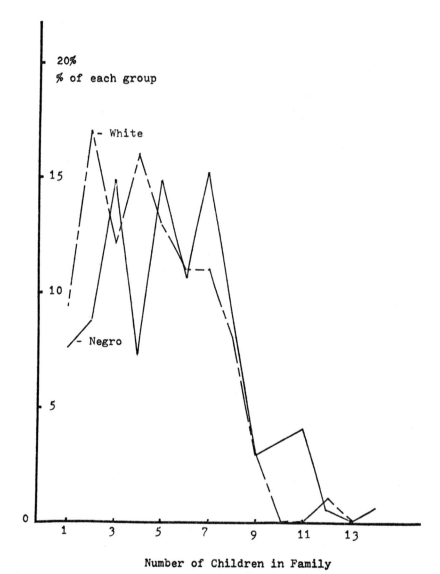

Number of Children in Family

FIGURE 19. *Comparison of white and Negro prisoners by size of family.* In both cases, there was a predominance of large families, the Negro families tending to be somewhat larger, in that 25 percent of whites but only 16 percent of Negroes came from families of two or less children.

warding experiences had been known. Contrariwise, and in contrast to predictions, a very popular option was, of all choices, "cosmetology," one expected to be the favorite only of effeminate males.

In the prison there was a wide variety of jobs available and assigned to prisoners according to abilities and to the status achieved in respect to "good behavior." The highest status jobs (from the prison administration's viewpoint) were clerical positions in the administrative offices. The few high school graduates tended to have these jobs, and although treasured by those who held them, did not appear to be particularly esteemed by the others. Perhaps the most widely sought after jobs in the least capable members of the prison population were those in food service. The attractions were based on the prospects for getting extra food, and on the prospects for being in a position of power in giving larger or smaller portions to other prisoners. Disciplinary problems were frequent among these workers, for perhaps similar reasons, as well as the occasion for prisoners getting their hands on weapons (butcher knives, etc.). Among the somewhat more capable prisoners, there was a high esteem for truck driving, apparently because these jobs often took the prisoner away from the prison when they delivered cargoes to other places. Large numbers of prisoners had no job assignments at all, but were irregularly organized in gangs for cleaning up the grounds, etc. These prisoners not infrequently manifested evidence of disappointing conflicts arising over these situations. In the first place, they often held the notion that the ability to survive without doing any work represented some sort of utopia. Once in such a situation, however, they were overpowered by the monotony and the sense of endless waiting for termination of their sentence—an unexpected lack of satisfaction for the predicted utopia.

In general, then, some of the notable conclusions that can be made from the relation of subjects to the world of work include: (a) a prevailing ignorance of occupational information; (b) an absence in their backgrounds of desirable models to follow in relation to work; (c) illusions about the blessings of living without working, and (d) unfamiliarity with the institu-

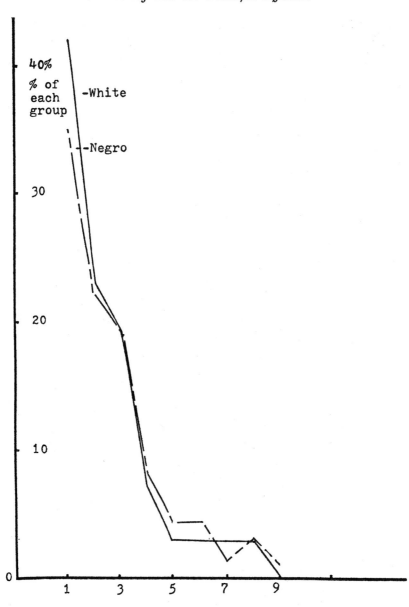

Position in Family

FIGURE 20. *Comparison of white and Negro prisoners by position in family.*
No difference of any significant degree is observable. Both groups tended
to come from large families, and in both groups there was a higher than
expected incidence of first -born.

tionalized procedures involved in the entry of youth into the labor force. As with other attitudes discussed, these observations about jobs and work add up to another *missing link* with conventional society, ordinarily not missing in other populations.

ATTITUDES TOWARD FRIENDS AND FRIENDSHIPS: A major source of internalized conflict was evident in the subjects' attitudes toward friendships. On the one hand, they had usually had the experience of having enjoyed some degree of acceptance by a group of their peers, and *apparently* because of this (but *really* because no one else had accepted them) this group represented an asset in their lives. On the other hand, it was almost always their relationship with the group which had brought about arrest and imprisonment. The police, the courts, their mothers, the prison officials consistently condemned these relationships as something which must be despised and terminated because continuation would certainly lead to future trouble. Although not inclined to be sympathetic with these views, substantiating evidence for them came from the frequency with which other group members had "squealed" on them, had failed to "alibi" for them, or had managed to get off with less severe punishments. Other prisoners condemned the other group members who had shared the previous delinquent behavior, not on the grounds of its having been "wrong" but because it had been done "stupidly."

The subjects consistently expressed these conflicts, for instance, by insisting that their "friends" were not "friends" but only "associates" (the street language called them "rap partners"). Only rarely were wives seen as friends, indicating that whatever friendships were used for did not include the roles which wives filled. Brothers, also, were rarely identified as friends. The test of friendship was trust, and although others were often entrusted with something valuable (lending money, sharing secrets of delinquent acts, etc.), the trust was more frequently than not violated. Strangely, some other people might have been considered trustworthy, but had not been included as potential friends because nothing of value had ever been entrusted to them (e.g. school teachers).

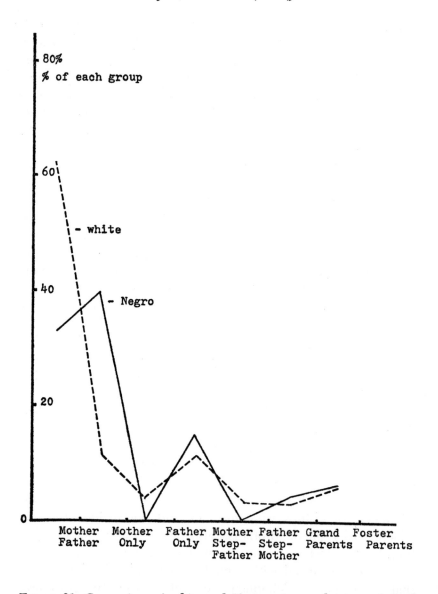

FIGURE 21. *Comparison of white and Negro prisoners by type of family leadership.* Significantly, more Negro (40%) than white (10%) prisoners came from families with no father. The estimates were made of the conditions prevailing during the five years preceding imprisonment. Balancing this disproportion, the whites had more mother-father combinations (62% vs. 35%). Remarkably few foster parents were present in the families.

BIRTH ORDER AND SOCIAL OUTCOME

There has long been a prevailing concept that first born children are more likely than their siblings to achieve success and recognition. H. A. Ellis in "A Study of British Genius" (1926) reported that of 1030 prominent Britons, 56 percent were first born. Ellis' criteria for selecting his subject population appeared to be based more on how widely known they were rather than how successful they were in other ways. J. M. Cattell, the editor of *American Men of Science*, pointed out as early as 1927 that 57.4 percent of the distinguished scientists listed in this directory were first born. Similarly, E. Huntingdon found that 64 percent of the people listed in Who's Who in 1938 were first born. W. F. Ogburn further observed that the youngest, as well as the oldest in the family tended to be over-represented in Who's Who (1927). L. M. Terman's "Genetic Studies of Genius" in 1925 reported the traits of 1000 unusually gifted children, of which 56.1 percent were first born. More recently, in 1965, W. D. Altus observed that 55 percent of 4,000 entering college students were first born ("Birth Order and Academic Primogeniture," Journal of Personality and Sociological Psychology). He further found that in families of two children, 68 percent of first born entered college, and in families of three children, 50 percent of the first born went to college. P. C. Capra and J. E. Dittes reported in 1962 that 61 percent of Yale undergraduates were first born. The likelihood of persons in the general population being first born is about 32 percent.

As prisoners approached the time of discharge from the prison, the issue of friendship with former members of the peer group, and of reinstating their relationship with them became prominent. The conflict tended to become more and more acute as the time approached when they would come into contact with them. One of the most remarkable phenomenon observed was the rarity of instances when they considered the neurotic solution to the conflict—by avoiding the situation. Instead, their plans almost invariably included coming face to face with the former friends in the old neighborhood. Somehow, they seldom seemed aware of the difficulties they would have to face there: the prejudice of the police and community at large, the problems with the former friends who had betrayed them, the known absence of opportunity, etc.

ATTITUDES TOWARD THE PRISON: The expected displeasure

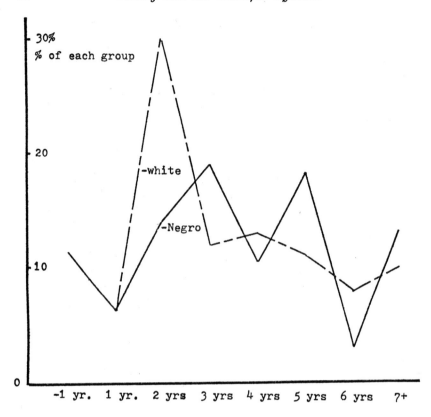

FIGURE 22. *Comparison of white and Negro prisoners by length of present sentence.* When the white and the Negro population is compared by distribution of prison sentences, there is evident a rather definite tendency for the latter to have been given longer ones. 60 percent of whites were given sentences for three years or less, whereas 50 percent of Negroes were given sentences of this magnitude, leaving 50 percent of Negroes and 40 percent of whites with longer sentences. Although it would be officially and vehemently denied to be the case, whites were more likely to get their sentences shortened by parole. On the other hand, it was found that more whites than Negroes refused parole, preferring, instead to leave prison unencumbered by the restrictions of parole supervision. This attitude seemed at first glance like a rather malignant one, indicating a lack of willingness to change former delinquency patterns. Nevertheless, it also appeared to represent a degree of constructive independence, too, by virtue of eliminating the application for parole as a bargaining level for the prison to exercise power over the offender.

and antagonism expressed toward the prison appeared to be more stereotyped and institutionalized than truly personal. In other words, it looked much like the ubiquitous complaints of the enlisted man toward the army that he was a part of. There was little evidence of deep bitterness or search for vengeance against the prison. On the other hand, there was little or no evidence that any sense of satisfaction was felt in being in the prison. The major riot which had taken place in the prison only a few months before had left a clear and deep impression on the prison administration, but seemed to have little or no repercussions among the prisoners. It was quite rare for a prisoner to express any great fear toward guards or other prison officials. On the contrary, fear was frequently expressed toward other prisoners who had a reputation for brutality. The complaints made against guards were about the sort one might expect to hear expressed by some high school students about teachers. Many of the guards had a widespread reputation among the prisoners for being fair and reasonably compassionate. A few, on the other hand, were known as very likely to arrive at rigid interpretations of the prison rules which could lead to prisoners being punished. Extra punishment could vary from denial of the privilege of attending a weekly movie to solitary confinement for weeks.

In a small but significant proportion of the prison population there could be found a certain pride in the prison itself. Members of the prison basketball team might show this pride, or the members of another group which had organized itself to build a large scale electrified model of a neighboring Civil War battlefield. When the new building complex mentioned above was opened, a revealing vignette was witnessed. In this case, one of the prisoners was showing his father around a new building with very evident pride. The father remarked, after being properly impressed: "They don't make these places the way they did when I was your age. When I was in the Georgia State Penitentiary thirty years ago . . ."

When their life experiences had been unfolded and when they then revealed that a large portion of their lives had been spent in correctional institutions, it was frequently pointed out

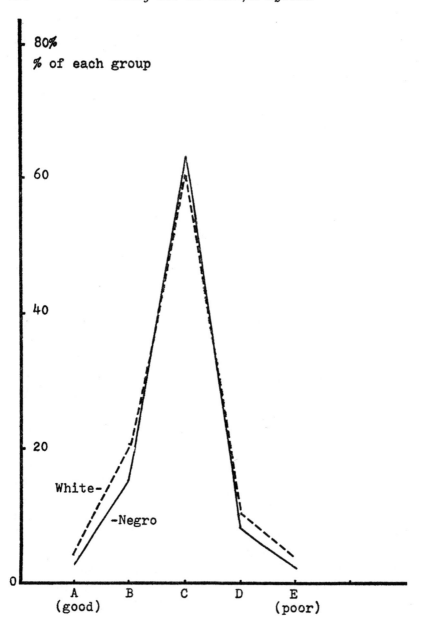

Level of Adjustment

FIGURE 23. *Comparison of white and Negro prisoners by level of prison adjustment.* No difference between the two groups can be noted. The prison

that since this was one subject that they must know a great deal about, it might be a good idea for them to think of working for such institutions. This kind of a proposition invariably elicited a string of vehement protests, indicating that nothing would interest them less. Similarly, they claimed it to be absolutely unthinkable that they could ever picture themselves working in any capacity related to law enforcement, courts, schools or any kind of institution.

Attitudes toward the prison constituted another source of potential conflict among the prisoners. On the one hand, the sentiments from and pressures exerted on them by their fellow prisoners demanded that they display consistently antagonistic and uncooperative attitudes toward the guards and the prison administration. In the face of the fellow prisoners, therefore, they dared not display any willingness to work, to obey rules or to please prison personnel. On the other hand, their status in respect to the prison administration, and closely associated with their prospects for parole, depended upon a display of a cooperative spirit toward the prison demands. Additional factors which could intensify the conflict was the occasional to frequent discovery that some of the guards or other officials were truly treating them with fairness and a reasonable degree of compassion. This was especially apt to be the case with the teachers in the prison school. In other words, as was the case with so many of their other experiences in life, their expectations—often dictated to them by their local culture—came in conflict with their own experiences. This kind of disillusionment might often conform to what conventional society would applaud, except that it served only to estrange them from the past, from their own interpersonal relationships, but without substituting anything in its place which could lead to greater trust in the social system.

Another phenomenon related to attitudes toward prison was common. In very many instances, either their expressed views

---

administration tended to see the Negro population as more troublesome than the whites, but this bias might have been due to the fact that there were three times more Negroes as whites.

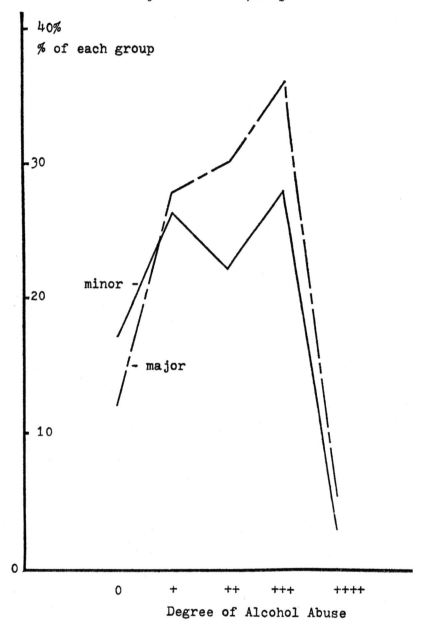

FIGURE 24. *Comparison of white and Negro prisoners by degree of alcohol-drug abuse.* More than twice as many Negro prisoners were abstainers than whites and nearly double the number of alcoholics were found among the whites. Drug problems did not differ between the two groups.

or their behavior indicated that when they had been enrolled in the public school system, it was looked upon as if it were a jail. The rules and regulations, and the demands made on them by teachers and principals created the image in their mind of what a prison would be like. However, now that they were actually in a prison, and perhaps not until the second or third time, they realized there was an enormous difference. Then, school did not look as bad as it had. In this case, the learned contrast between the reality of prison and that of school tended to improve their level of sophistication. However, in another instance similar comparisons had the opposite effect. Toward the end of their school careers they would tend to look forward to escape from school through taking jobs as a route to freedom. In the prison, however, working on a job was equated with being a *good* prisoner, and thus, work tended to get all mixed up with attitudes toward imprisonment. Furthermore, work was demanded of them as a condition of staying out of prison, a demand which they tended to resent, perhaps because they could not genuinely deny its truth. The institutionalization of work which they had already encountered and had probably already failed to cope with successfully (e.g. getting to work on time, working every day, etc.) began to look as demanding to them as either school in the past or prison in the present. At best, then, work had only negative incentives (e.g. means of avoiding punishment).

TYPICAL CHARACTEROLOGICAL PICTURE

From the collection of the qualitative and quantitative data obtained on the offender population, a *typical* subject might be described, from the point of view of his life history and characterological development. The example to be described would fit a substantially large share of the total population, and this *typical* example would constitute the *common person*, the *average citizen*, of this population. As such, it would be lacking in the more dramatic and vivid pictures which might be, nevertheless, quite applicable to other smaller groups in the population, which by virtue of their greater degrees of conspicuousness to others are more likely to be seen as representative.

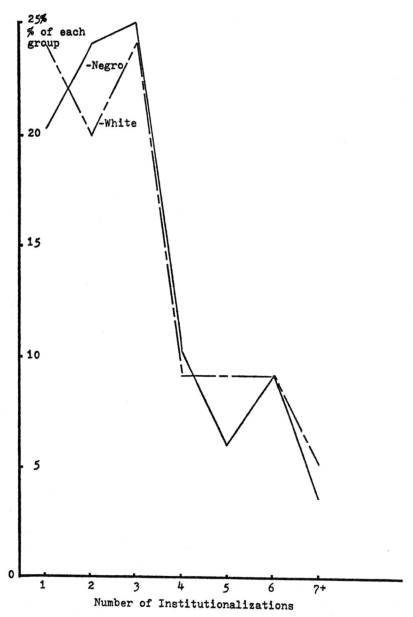

FIGURE 25. *Comparison of white and Negro prisoners in frequency of insti-tutionalization.* A marked similarity is evident in the two populations, with both having experienced a high incidence of previous institutionalizations. The institutions in which prisoners had previously been committed included

In the first place, they probably would not look very much, if at all, different from another group from the same socio-economic background (big city ghetto) who had dropped out of school early, was working in non-skilled jobs but who had no record of anti-social offenses. The typical case was a boy from a large family in which the father was an absent or very shadowy figure and in which both he and the mother were migrants from the rural south with little education and no occupational skills. The typical boy was quite passive, dependent on mother and deprived of any substantial male adult models who had any influence on him (meaning, probably, that no significant male adult had ever shown any interest in him). He had no family tradition to provide guidance for behavior, and the passivity of the mother was such that no significant set of approvals or disapprovals from her offered any measurable guide. This typical boy drifted passively and indolently through elementary school with very little impact of one on the other. When he reached his adolescent years, he became associated with a small group of peers, who showed enough interest in him that he thereby became influenced by their expectations. Existence became more than mere survival after this. For the first time, he found an understandable model to follow, conformity to which brought social acceptance from the peer group and a chance to find a mode of self-expression. For the most part, this consisted of an exhibitionistic demonstration of an adolescent concept of masculinity and self-assertiveness. Conformity to the group's expectations was simple to understand, whereas the more subtle expectations of society at large were both incomprehensible and productive of no recognizable incentive, since no rewards from the greater society were offered or even made to look desirable. Conformity to the peer group's expectations required a disdain of schooling and experimentation with sex,

---

state training schools (*reform schools*), other jails and prisons, this prison, and state hospitals. In only a very small number of cases did previous institutionalizations include placement outside the state. In only 24 percent of whites and 20 percent of Negroes was the present prison sentence the only institutionalization experienced. A higher percentage of each had four or more institutionalizations.

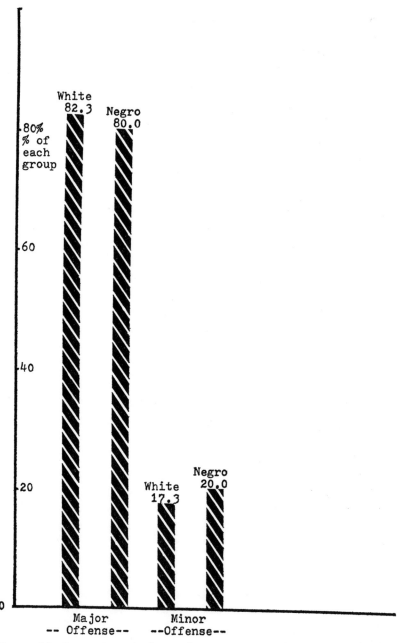

FIGURE 26. *Comparison of white and Negro prisoners by major versus minor crimes.* As can be seen, there is not significant difference. Nevertheless, the Negro subjects tended to have been given longer sentences, as illustrated in FIGURE 14.

alcohol and stealing. Only immediate, visible pleasure served as a motive for work. Marriage, having a home of one's own, material possessions of long-range value, had no value and, therefore, demanded no preparation. During his adolescent years, he spent most of his time with his group in rather aimless socializing, conducting himself with them in accordance with their naive concepts of being adult and male. The offenses for which members of the group would be arrested and imprisoned were not distinguished, particularly from their other tests of territorial boundaries, which did not carry the risk of arrest. During his brief interludes at home, he would be generally uncommunicative, indolent, and quite childish in his behavior. Arrest and conviction was considered to be proof of masculine assertiveness, on the one hand, but also a product of stupidity.

"Getting away with something" illegal carried with it such high status, that he might make false confessions of offenses, or fail to provide himself with adequate defense in court. The people with whom he had some contact, who behaved differently, and with whom he could contrast his behavior would be almost entirely women whom he regarded as living lives of drudgery, and not with successful men who enjoyed the fruits of freedom, education and acceptance in the larger society. His closest contacts with the society outside his world were local merchants and neighborhood policemen, for whom he could muster no respect or envy. He saw little in their lives which appealed to him, and although the pleasure seeking he was engaged in was more illusory than real, it seemed attainable.

In spite of frequent contacts with school teachers, he did not look upon them as models. Childishly, he saw fate and fortune as made up of good or bad luck, over which he exercised little control, so that no need was felt for any preparation for the future. With this fatalism, he could face failure with a measure of good humor and foresaw no long-term disadvantages to arrest and imprisonment. Only the greater society outside has attached a measure of disapproval to prison records. It would take him several years before he found out how a bad record could serve as a handicap, for he did not yet consider desirable those pathways (military service, responsible jobs, etc.) for which a prison record served as an obstacle.

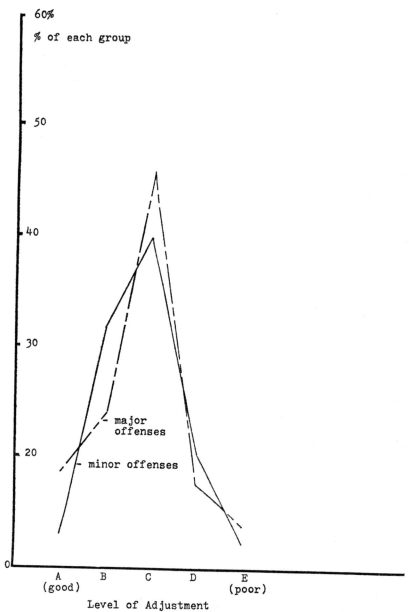

FIGURE 27. *Comparison of prisoners with major versus those with minor offenses in respect to level of prison adjustment.* A general, qualitative impression gained in studying the prison population leads one to the conclusion that the major offenders make better prison adjustments than the minor

The outstanding characteristic of his life which precipitated his arrests and imprisonments coincided, contradictorily, with his only experiences in life which were pleasant and exciting to him. Both resulted from his acceptance into a gang which showed him the way to status and independence through irresponsible pleasure-seeking activities. In spite of the disastrous consequences of ending up in prison through these activities, they still represented his sole motivation for behavior, and, as a result, a major barrier toward his directing his future activities into more responsible and socially acceptable directions. Only after repeated institutionalizations did he become disillusioned with the heavy price he had to pay for these activities, yet had no other models to follow. He had learned to survive in a restricted world which demanded no preparations for the future, and in which all emphasis was placed on the visible and the immediate. Home represented a source of protection and warmth in the person of a passive, tolerant mother; but no leadership and no adult model of responsible masculinity were present. In short, his experiences and training adapted him solely for a brief period of rather wild, reckless, pleasure-seeking adolescence after which he was left with no incentives, goals, objectives, or skills.

The offenses for which these subjects were arrested were often accidental consequences of careless, irresponsible actions rather than deliberate attempts to be destructive or anti-social. In most cases, it could be safely stated that if the subject had stayed at home in bed on a certain day of his life, he might not have ended up in prison. He always knew other youths who had seemed immune to the punitive consequences of delinquency, and was inclined to be confident of his own immunity.

Purse-snatching, shop-lifting and other examples of theft were activities he equated with other experiments with growing up, such as smoking, drinking and sexual adventures. Although he sensed a general disapproval of these activities by people

---

offenders. This conclusion is supported to only a slight degree by these distribution curves. In the case of the best adjustment (A), for instance, substantially more of the major offenders are represented, but otherwise the differences between the two groups is not very remarkable.

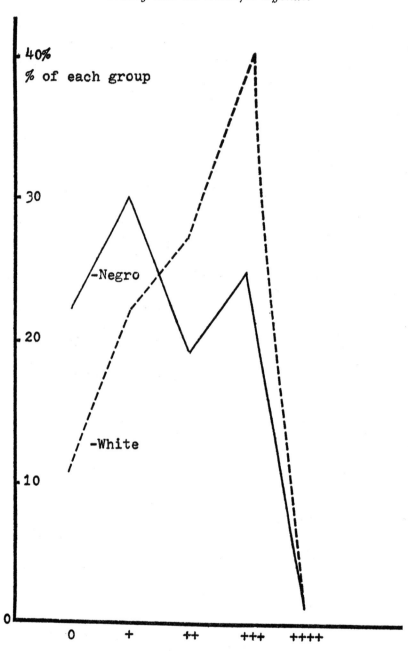

Degree of Alcohol-Drug Abuse

outside his culture (school teachers, etc.), he failed to distinguish, for instance, the disapproval against smoking and disapproval against stealing. He might be reprimanded for smoking in school, for instance, but this was no great tragedy, even if repeated offenses led to his being expelled. As far as he was concerned, he "got away with it." Playing truant from school or shop-lifting during early adolescence might result in his going to the Boys' Training School for a few months, but this was not looked upon as a disaster, either. When, however, he passed the age of 16, the same kind of offenses resulted in arrest and imprisonment; he had great difficulty comprehending the different significance which society attached to these offenses in the older boys. Similarly, he might be arrested for street fighting, which he and his peers regarded as private matters that did not touch society at large, and would be vastly disillusioned to find himself in jail for these experiences. Above all, he was intimately acquainted with numerous examples of other offenses of the same sort which went unnoticed and unpunished, preserving for him the easy conviction that he could "get away with" them also. Failure to "get away with" them was merely bad luck which could not be anticipated, however.

In brief, this young man finally arrives in prison during late adolescence with a sense of self-identification only beginning to crystallize, with little concept of having any control over his own destiny and with relatively little incentive to pursue any but immediate and often illusory goals. Most of his concepts of the greater society had been formed by contacts with welfare and law enforcement institutions, and those institutions other people tend to rely on are still quite unfamiliar to him.

CHARACTEROLOGICAL DISTINCTIONS OF SMALLER SUB-GROUPS

The sub-group which, perhaps, comes closest to a popular public image of the *juvenile delinquent* differs quite markedly from the typical representative of the majority group. The arro-

FIGURE 28. *Comparison of white and Negro prisoners by degree of alcohol-drug abuse.* About twice as many whites as Negroes were serious alcohol problems.

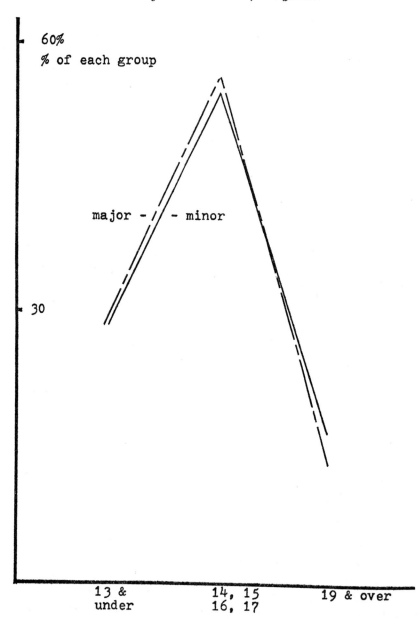

FIGURE 29. *Distribution of major versus minor offenders by age of first offense.*
The similarities belie the common assumption that offenders escalate the

gance, brashness and rebelliousness often expected of the entire offender population is actually characteristic of only a small number. However, because this smaller group is louder, more expressively verbal and more dramatic, it is much more likely than the larger group to attract attention, and become the object of studies which rely on greater communication skills for their data. The old psychiatric diagnostic category "psychopath," or the newer "sociopath" is applicable to this group. A striking distinguishing characteristic, different from the larger group, is that its population is, much less than the other, a function of social class. In other words, its members are not found nearly as exclusively in the lower socio-economic, disinfranchised urban ghetto segment of the population. In the total offender population studied, not more than about 10 percent of the total could properly be placed in this category.

In contrast to the other group, a study of the life histories of this sub-group would lead the investigator to predict that ultimate trouble with the law would be an inevitable, rather than chance outcome. Whereas the type of treatment accorded the first group by family, then by school and society in general was best characterized as neglect—being ignored mostly—the psychopath was most often treated at home with aggressive, exploitative domination and often cruelty. To this he tended to react with rebellion, and by carrying a general attitude of rebellion over to the expectations made on him by agencies outside the home, ended up getting into trouble. Furthermore, his troubles tended, more than the other group, to snowball, in that each unfortunate experience tended to create the seeds of a repetition of the same thing. A useful analogy would be to state that the larger group had led lives in an environment characterized by anarchy—a leaderless, dependent, passive environment in which could be found little in the way of incentive for achieving anything. The sub-group in question, however, came from a tyrannical environment which provoked aggressive, re-

---

severity of their crimes over time, so that those with major offenses would be assumed to have started earlier. Instead, there is no significant difference in the two groups by age of first offense.

bellious counter reactions—these offering the basis, at least, for a definite incentive, although more often destructive than constructive.

These youths tended to be more alert, intelligent and better informed, although they were just as likely as the others to have terminated their schooling without having profited much from it. Because, also, they were more verbal, as well as both interested in and adept at exploiting others (as they had been ex-

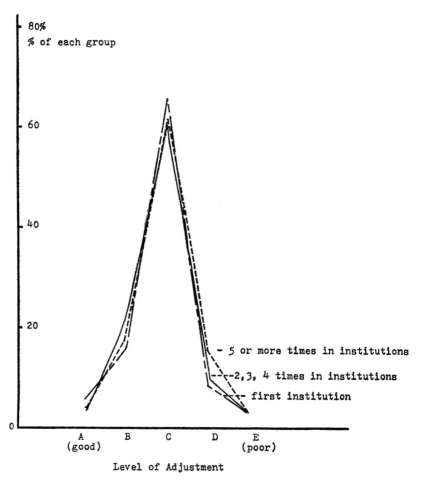

FIGURE 30. *Comparison of groups according to how many times they have been institutionalized, by level of prison adjustment.* Those with more institutionalizations showed neither better nor worse levels of adjustment.

ploited), they often became the leaders of the street gang. Even within this group, a hierarchial set of distinctions was evident, with the more violent-prone ones (the bullies) at the bottom of the list, and the "confidence artist" at the top. The latter group tended to exploit the prison situation with some success through the expertise they developed in being "jailwise" (knowing the art of making favorable impressions on the prison administration). The former group did so by bullying the more passive prisoners to do their bidding.

It is interesting to note that the corrections and related literature are most likely to cite examples of delinquent behavior in the form of the case histories of this type of offender. Also, the remarkable ability some of them often acquire in *conning* others is responsible for many of the enthusiastic but misleading claims of reform and rehabilitation.

Psychiatrists, parole officers, social workers and other people who often make long-term efforts to re-socialize these youths become very pessimistic with increasing experience with them, because of the frequency with which they present an initial appearance of being motivated to make favorable changes only to end up disappointing anyone interested in helping them. In other words, it is not merely the frequency of unfavorable outcomes that generates pessimistic prognoses, but, also the frequency with which *hope* for a favorable outcome is initially instilled. The ability to *con* others, coupled with their marked proclivity to avoid living up to anyone else's expectations yields these consequences. Other problem youths may not generate so much disappointment simply because less hope is held out for them to begin with.

Nevertheless, there is a way to cope with this group of offenders which can achieve results which fall short of total disaster. Rather than approaching them on the grounds of changing for the sake of others, for moral reasons or in the interest of becoming socially acceptable, another appeal can have more impact. In the first place, considerable allowance must be made for their continuing to lead a life which is unconventional, although still not necessarily anti-social to a degree which could lead to subsequent trouble with the law. By presenting to them

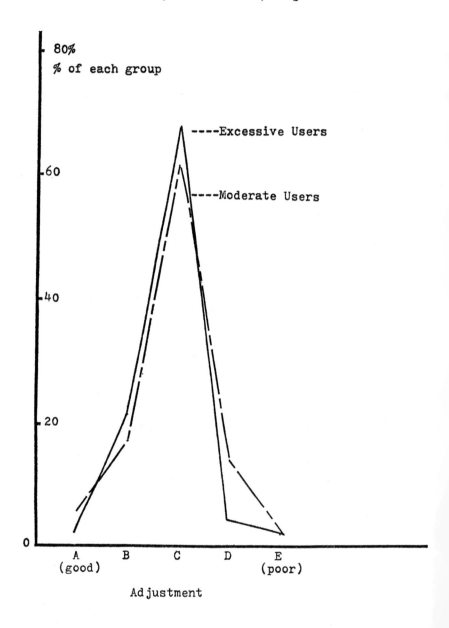

FIGURE 31. *Comparison of excessive versus moderate users of alcohol by level of prison adjustment.* As can be seen, no difference between the two groups is evident.

a plan which can successfully keep them out of the clutches of the law, their interest and cooperation can be excited, but in the process they can often be trapped into achieving this by being law-abiding, even though unconventional. To do this requires that they find an environment having a minimum of institutionalized restrictions and maximum freedom for conducting their lives in an unconventional way. Above all, the dangers they are most likely to encounter must be avoided, and that is the opportunity to exploit others who are susceptible to exploitation.

Another, still smaller, sub-group was found to be made up of rather straight forward neurotic types. In these, the delinquent behavior which had led to brushes with the law was an expression of a deep-seated neurotic conflict; often, for instance, taking the form of trying to shame or disgrace their parents. One example, for instance, was in prison for the third time, each time having been for a major crime; and, the latest was for armed robbery and attempted murder. In each of these three offenses, however, the victim of each crime was his father!

Typically, instead of the apathy characteristic of the first and largest group, and of the hostility of the second group described, the neurotic group members exhibited the predominant feature of fear. They were, contradictorily, inclined to be fearful of public disapproval, in spite of their occasional experiences with anti-social conduct. They were more likely than the others to have been married and to have used illegal means to support their family. They would tend to make rather elaborate efforts to establish relationships with the investigator, as well as with others who might prove helpful to them. Characteristically, however, these relationships would often encounter the contradiction of seeking a dependent role on the one hand while resisting the obligations of dependency on the other. Their plans for the future were likely to sound more constructively thought out, although just as likely to end up in indecision. Clearly, this group, although quite small in number, represented a salvageable portion of the offender population, if reliable guidance could be provided them. The solution is to help them find less self-defeating ways of living.

A tiny group, existing on the fringes of the prison popula-

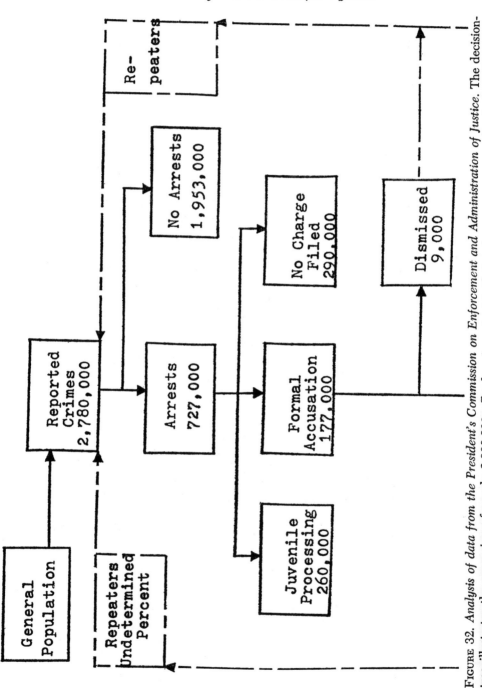

Figure 32. *Analysis of data from the President's Commission on Enforcement and Administration of Justice. The decision-*
tree illustrates the screening of nearly 3,000,000 offenders in respect to their subsequent encounters with the enforcement

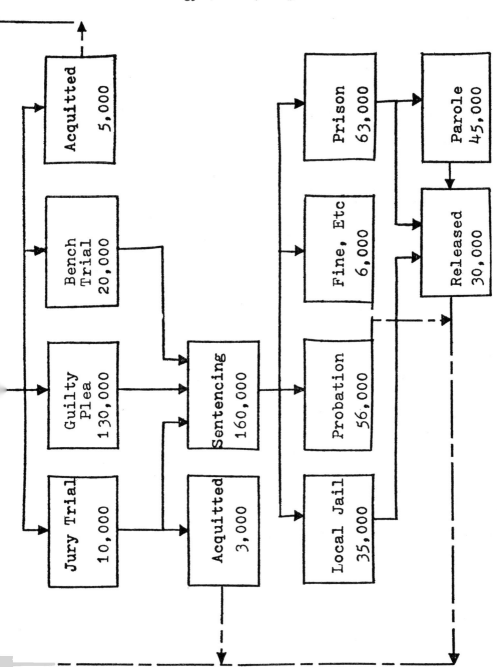

tion, and one which originated from the fringes outside the prison was also of note. This group was made up of essentially homeless, abandoned young men who had spent most of their lives in institutions, beginning with orphanages. They tended to be markedly uneducated, illiterate, and essentially mentally retarded. They generally seemed helpless and harmless to anyone who encountered them. Not uncommonly, it was evident that they were in prison mostly because the courts did not know what else to do with them. In the prison, they were the frequent victims of bullying by other prisoners, but also as frequently protected by prison personnel.

Perhaps the most outstanding feature of the final sub-group to be mentioned was how small, rather than how large its membership was. This group was made up of what, in psychiatric circles would be probably classified as "simple schizophrenia." The rigors of prison, one would suppose, would tend to provoke more psychotic behavior than was actually found. The author of this report has also had occasion to have made a study of a German concentration camp population (WWII), where even more serious stress was exerted on the resident population; but there, too, psychotic behavior was remarkable for its rarity (though present). This last sub-group exhibited the life histories of the typical schizophrenic, and this frequently included institutionalization in the past in mental hospitals. The crimes of which they had been convicted were sometimes bizarre ones (e.g. murdering attempts toward their father), but more often rather simple ones such as shop-lifting. They had not usually been a member of a street gang, and usually had very limited support from people on the outside.

CHAPTER VI

THE PRISON SOCIETY AND THE OFFENDERS

THE YOUTHFUL OFFENDER IN PRISON

FEW, IF ANY, public institutions are as little known by the public as are correctional institutions. Knowledge about the conditions prevailing in jails, prisons, hospitals for the criminally insane, and "reform schools" is well known to the offenders who inhabit them and the prison personnel who work in them, but by very few additional people. The families of prisoners see a tiny bit of prison life when they visit inmates, as do their defense attorneys, and occasional policemen who bring them to prison.

The vast majority of the American citizenry, however, the taxpayers whose money supports the system, have never had occasion to see any more than might be visible from a nearby highway and develop their notions from the distortions they see on T.V. Most important of all, perhaps, little is known of the prisons by the state legislators and federal congressmen who pass the laws or by the courts and juries which enforce them. It might well be a worthwhile part of the indoctrination of all judges of criminal courts that they spend some minimum period of time in a prison before they are ever allowed to sentence someone there, and at least one particular, responsible committee of each legislature should become equally familiar with prisons.

Because the public (including juries, legislatures, etc.) is almost completely unaware of the conditions that prevail in prisons, or the nature of the actual experiences of an inmate, they are only too free to raise the hue and cry which demands that prisons be kept filled, and that new ones be built. Their demands are made with apparent inpunity because when the offender is sent away to a prison for a few years, he is safely away from the society outside which might otherwise be attentive to his plight.

It is evident that the structure, appurtenances and administration of the total law enforcement system have been expensively designed and equipped to cope with a criminal population that it only rarely encounters. Actually, the vast majority of enforcement effort is directed toward a very different assortment of social problems manifested by minor traffic violations, alcoholics, juvenile delinquency, and large numbers of private morals offenses and petty thefts.

The latter populations differ markedly from those which the system has been designed to cope with in the sense that their threats to society are individually of an entirely different order than are those supposed to be posed by the destructiveness of the "hardened criminal" or organized crime. An example is evident in the observation that policemen universally are equipped with large caliber lethal weapons which could prove very effective in dealing with the "hardened criminal," but become, instead, extraordinarily dangerous when coping with the more usual traffic law offender, or juvenile, or alcoholic. Similarly, the typical prison with its elaborate security system effectively protects society from, perhaps, 10 percent of the population housed there, while exposing the other 90 percent to the very influences which they are supposedly being removed from by imprisonment.

THE PRISON SYSTEM

In the book *After Conviction: A New Review of the American Correctional System* by Robert Goldfarb and Linda Singer (Simon & Schuster, 1972) the authors report on the results of an extensive study they conducted of the prison system. For instance, in response to their inquiry, nearly all of the correctional officials stated that not more than 10 to 20 percent of the present prison inmates needed to be there for the protection of society. The authors concluded that the system is a 200 year old experiment which has failed, and many of the corollary parts of the system were originated in the U.S., to be exported around the world. At the present time, the enforced confinement of the offender within prison walls for a prescribed period of time is the central core of the system of crime deterrance — sometimes used as a threat, othertimes as a reality. The original American prisons, operated in Philadelphia by the Quakers, then at Auburn, New York, also imposed complete isolation from others while in prison in order to facilitate their communion with God and subsequent salvation. This practice was abandoned as the number of psychotic breakdowns and suicides became alarming. Practically all modifications of the system since then have still retained, however, the essential feature of enforced confinement. The failures in the system as a deterrant to crime, therefore, have been universal, regardless of the modification used, and could be attributed to this one common denominator. For instance, even today the prison with adequate space and active rehabilitation programs has as high a rate of recidivism as the ones which are overcrowded and have no rehabilitation program. The process of institutionalizing large numbers of similar kinds of maladjusted people for considerable periods of time, whether in a prison or in a mental hospital, appears to have uniformly disappointing effects. It now seems evident that the rich manage rather consistently to avoid imprisonment for wrong-doing and are less likely to be repeaters. The poor populate the prisons, and consistently show a high repeat rate. The difference may not be that of economics, but of the effects of institutionalization.

The preoccupation of the personnel staffing the enforcement system with the relatively harmless offenders which take up most of their time is understandable, for the tough offenders who are the real threats to society are very dangerous and unpleasant people. The latter are more likely than the others to possess the shrewdness and resources which make them capable of outwitting the system, as well, and although dangerous and numerous enough to justify a great deal of law enforcement attention, actually attract only a small percentage of it.

An important facet of the society within the prison that the public at large is likely to be unaware of is that it is truly a society—a complete society. The prisoners do not, as the public seems to assume, merely go into some sort of hibernation while awaiting the end of their sentences. Instead, they live a full life, not too much different than the one they lived outside, except that they are given no responsibility and are reasonably well fed. Outside, they are confronted with responsibility, but often or always manage to avoid it. Inside they are not even confronted with it. As a society, the prison life is made up of individual and group relations which are both constructive and destructive. There are feuds, friendships, loves (even marriages), thefts, murders, swindles, hopes, fears, sicknesses, work, leisure time, entertainment, loafing, and even some politics, religion and education.

ATTICA AND AFTER

Following the bloody riots in the New York prison at Attica, the American Assembly, arranged by Columbia University, devoted its attention to the question of the American prison systems in its 1972 meeting. There was general agreement that an immediate change in the system which was called for was a dramatic decrease in the kind and number of offenders placed in local, state and federal prisons, Clearly, imprisonment in these institutions has done more harm than good. Perhaps not more than 10 to 20 percent of the present prison population properly belong in institutions on the grounds of protecting society. Furthermore, drastic changes in the enforcement system and in the respect for law and order could be brought about by "decriminalizing many of the current "victimless" crimes (alcohol, drugs, gambling, vagrancy, homesexuality). As one participant stated: "We must stop loading down our criminal justice system with huge numbers of cases involving moral improprieties." The vast sums of money spent on expensive new institutions could better be spent on other components of the system.

The youthful offender is somewhat different in respect to the potential impact which the prison society might have on him from an older adult who might be there for the first time. In the case of the youth, who is serving a sentence of a few years, and especially if he has already served previous sentences also, he will have, thereby, spent a very substantial portion of his total post-child life in that society. As a consequence, a large proportion of his total knowledge and skills will be made up of what he learned in that society.

For those youths who have, by the time they are 25 or so spent a half or more of their lives since puberty in institutions, it is no surprise to find that they become, thereby, suited for very little else except to continue the same life which leads back to prison. A picture of the significance of these observations can be envisaged by hypothesizing two different young men. One might imagine one, middle class youth with a conventional life and background who spends the four years between age 18 and 22 going to college. Another youth might be imagined who has the typical disharmonious family and deprived environmental background of the common youthful prisoner, but who spends the four years between age 18 and 22 serving a prison sentence. When the two face the adult world at the end of this period, each has an entirely different set of skills, values and fund of knowledge to solve life's problems with. It is almost inconceivable that the first would do anything except end up succeeding and the other end up failing to make the conventional, socially acceptable decisions which society expects. Only the first one has an investment in the "Establishment" and some guarantees that he can get out of life what he wants by conventional means. The second has no investment to protect and no reason for feeling any confidence that conventional methods will get him what he desires in life.

Whether the prison is knowingly designed and operated as an educational experience for the inmates or not, the fact is that it will inevitably become one. It becomes an educational experience for the youthful offender because of the factors mentioned above. As such, the role in the prisoner's life of the society inside the prison is worthy of a broader examination than is usually accorded it. Society's choice is not *whether or not educational opportunities will be made available,* but only *what kind.* By default, prison society under the control of its inmates will write the curriculum, one on which might or might not be superimposed another curriculum written by prison administrators.

THE YOUTHFUL OFFENDER'S STATE AT ONSET OF PERIOD OF SENTENCE: The most striking quality of the state of affairs present in the offender when he arrives at the prison to serve his sentence is that of disillusionment. At no time during the period when he was outside did he expect to be there in prison, even though he might have been engaging in frequent activities which could inevitably lead to this outcome. His disillusionment is not directed toward himself, toward his own judgment or decision-making, for his sense of responsibility has never gone so far that he sees the outcome of life as a product of his own actions. Instead, he is disillusioned about the people he thought were his friends, but who betrayed him. He is disillusioned about his family and/or his attorney for not having won him acquittal. He is disillusioned about the whole social system which lets other people go free (he thinks) while he gets caught, for doing the same things. Typically, his disillusionment is likely to take the form of hostility, resentment, and distrust of others rather than depression. He is likely, then, to express these attitudes by a "chip on the shoulder" attitude when he arrives. However, nothing changes quicker than this, for there are too many people in the prison society ready to knock off this chip, and these people include both officials and fellow prisoners.

The new arrival has had experiences before when he has invaded the *turf* of rival youths, and comes to the prison expecting to encounter similar territorial problems. Consequently, he will be very alert to the detection of danger spots in his new environment, hopeful of finding some haven of protection and especially careful in concealing any vulnerability he might have. Unlike the more neurotic forms of maladjustment, his style will generally include the establishment of relationships for mutual protection. Thus, he is vulnerable, unwittingly, as he had been before, to the exploitation of the bully or the *con* man. Contradictorily, the intensity of his distrust of others is matched by an equal intensity of need to find someone to trust.

RECIDIVISM

The most striking fact about offenders who have been convicted of crimes is how often how many of them continue committing crimes . . . A review of a number of (such) studies in the various States and in the Federal prison system leads to the conclusion that despite considerable variation among jurisdictions, roughly a third of the offenders released from prison will be reimprisoned, usually for committing new offenses, within a 5-year period. The most frequent recidivists are those who commit such property crimes as burglary, auto theft, forgery or larceny, but robbers and narcotics offenders also repeat frequently. Those who are least linely to commit new crimes of violence: murder, rape and aggravated assault.

The Challenge of Crime in a Free Society, The President's Commission on Law Enforcement and the Administration of Justice, Government Printing Office, 1967.

When different kinds of people make up a given society, the influence each has on the behavior of the group is dependent upon certain obvious factors. In the first place, the numbers in each of the sub-groups will play a determining role, with a tendency for the sub-group having the largest number to have the greatest influence. Power plays another part, such that the sub-group with the greatest power to either reward or punish will have a determining influence. Ability to communicate and access to means of communication will also influence the relative influences of different sub-groups. Lastly, the expectations held by individual members of the society will help determine how they are influenced by others, in keeping with whether or not others meet their expectations.

The newly arrived prisoner will be confronted by the various sets of influences exercised by the different groups present in prison society, and will be affected according to these propositions. His own expectations are likely to be limited to a few very discrete and limited goals. In the first place, he will want to get out as soon as possible, and this expectation will color to a major degree the way in which the group influences he encounters will affect him. Concerning the influence which the prison officials might have on him, it is reasonably certain that he will have no expectations of ever seeing them again, or having anything to do with them, so is not likely to see any future in any good they can do him, except to help him get out. While he is there, he will be initially concerned, not with establishing long-term friendships, but with simple, straightforward physical safety. The influence, therefore, of those who can do harm is potentially very important, but more likely of a negative than positive nature (learning what not to do, learning how to protect oneself).

In respect to the issue of numbers of sub-groups members which he will come in contact with, he will be relating to fellow prisoners a hundred times more often than to prison officials, so that the influence of the former will have a marked dominance sheerly in terms of numbers of experiences. The issue of power will be a conflicting one for him, for both his fellow prisoners and the prison officials will appear to have almost life-and-death power over him, but the expectations of one will be contrary to the other. His mode of dealing with this power will have a determining influence on his life in prison. In respect to the communication links which might influence his behavior, there is most likely going to be a one-way flow to him with little feedback from him. His own passivity and ineptness in communications will render him relatively powerless in controlling or guiding it in his interests.

In order for some constructive, rehabilitative influence to be brought significantly to bear on the prisoner, whatever is offered will be in competition with other influences pointing in very different directions, few of which are likely to be constructive. In other words, the youthful offender, when in the prison environment, will be subjected to forces that tend to mold his behavior, but which are a by-product of the institution itself. Thus, "institutionalitis" or the dependency-producing tendency of the institution, will tend to have an increasingly accumulative effect. Over time, its influences come to be the most significant ones to which the inmate has to react, to cope, and to adjust to. In this environment, successful adjustment is feasible, but when successful, is applicable only to the problems of adjustment to an institution. Similar problems pertain to the patients in mental hospitals where there is seen a progressive loss, over time, of any skills in adjustment—tenuous to begin with—to the outside, non-institutional environment. Specifically, the "inside" differs from the "outside" in an all-encompassing way. On the "inside," the individual's decisions are made for him by the institution. On the "outside" he has to make his own. The ability to adjust to the one environment has very little carry-over in learning to cope with the other.

THE SANCTIONS OF THE INSTITUTION: Another facet of the

prisoner's experience which is likely to be unknown to the public at large, and not even faced as such by the system itself is the total impact of the social sanctions imposed by imprisonment. The public would be inclined to assume that it is merely a temporary deprivation of the freedom of mobility which is imposed on the prisoner. Actually, the action by the court of declaring him guilty of a crime and committing him to prison carries, at least, the following sanctions:

1. Not only is the prisoner denied the freedom of moving about the country according to his own wishes in accordance with the civil rights of other citizens, but he is denied, thereby, the freedom to make any of his own decisions which are dependent upon time or place. Thus, he is denied the freedom of choosing his friends or fellow workers, or type of work, of relationships with family, of contacts with *rational* society, etc.

2. He is denied the right to vote, to sign wills and contracts or checks or even to get in touch with anyone of his own choosing, other than his attorney.

3. He is denied the right to due process of law, in spite of the fact that he enjoyed this right until the moment he was found guilty. Thus, he has no constitutionally guaranteed route through which he can legally protect himself against all sorts of illegal exploitation, except the ill-defined guarantee that he is immune from "cruel and unusual punishment" (and then it is mostly his dubious credibility opposed to official credibility which protects him against this infringement of his freedom). Even when he is on probation or on parole, outside the prison, he is denied the right of due process, meaning that he can be sent back to prison by the decision of a single probation officer (for infraction of a rule that might be as minor as staying out after dark). The absence of protection by due process means, also, that in addition to the original punishment of imprisonment imposed on him by the court, the prison officials can now arbitrarily impose new measures, worst of which could be to confine him to solitary confinement as additional punishment.

4. The right of freedom of assembly and of free speech, and the corollary one of freedom of the press is denied him, and

these denials of freedom are consistent and nearly universal in prisons. What he can read or what letters he receives can, and is, controlled by someone else.

5.   The right to privacy is about as completely removed as it is possible to do so, and this denial of privacy includes his correspondence, which is typically censored. Only with his attorney does he enjoy any guarantee of confidentiality, and the likelihood of the typical youthful offender having an attorney of his own choosing and who is dedicated to his interest is a remote one.

6.   Strangely, perhaps, the one civil right which is least attenuated is his freedom of religion . . . a freedom which few offenders would know or care how to use in their own interests.

IMPLICATIONS OF LOSS OF CIVIL RIGHTS: Throughout the history of Anglo-Saxon jurisprudence, there has evolved a lengthening list of different kinds of people who are denied the set of rights ordinarily thought to be granted to all. For instance, a person must first be able to prove he is a citizen of the country before the traditional constitutional rights are tendered. Secondly, he must also be able to demonstrate that he is of suitable age, so that youths under the age of 18 (formerly 21), are in no way guaranteed any of the precious civil rights of Americans. Thirdly, he must be not adjudged mentally incompetent—a state of affairs that often occurs automatically on commitment to a mental hospital. And, lastly, he is denied his civil rights if he has been found guilty of a crime.

As the list of these disinfranchised people has grown over the centuries, it has become apparent that the effect on the individual of having been denied his civil rights is to place other people in a position where they make decisions for him. Thus, he comes under the control of others, and it does not take long before it becomes evident that others sometimes abuse this power. Therefore, our courts have gradually provided safeguards designed to protect the disinfranchised person against the abuse of power which others thereby gain over him. Society has come to expect that those in these positions of power demonstrate some reasonable degree of accountability for the responsibility they end up with.

Once it is considered how great and how extensive the power of the correctional system has over the prisoner through the right it has to make nearly all his decisions for him, it should, but seldom does, raise the important question of how this should be carried out in the interest of all concerned. In other words, once the prison has received the prisoner under its care for a given period of time, what responsibility does it now have to society and to the prisoner? Prison officials can be censured for failure to prevent escapes, and very rarely they might be slapped on the wrists when accused of "cruel and unusual punishment," but are rarely held accountable for anything else. Murders take place in prison with great regularity, but without much scrutiny being attracted from the outside. Riots are also regular occurrences; and these, too, can be very bloody affairs, but not until Attica has any appreciable amount of attention been attracted to the system which spawns them.

Mental hospitals, orphanages and nursing homes are other examples of institutions where the inmates come under the complete control of a system which makes their decisions for them. Substantial inroads have been made into the traditional immunity from censure which these institutions heretofore enjoyed. As a result, increasingly effective accountability measures are being introduced to curb the abuse of power which thereby becomes possible. Little in this direction, however, has happened with prison administration. To a large degree, this failure is due to the general state of ignorance which prevails in the public about the prison society.

THE EDUCATIONAL ENVIRONMENT OF THE PRISON: Even the most vengeful segment of the general population, those who see the prison as serving solely a punitive function, would not advocate that prisoners be taught new or more entrenched anti-social attitudes and skills. If punishment is to serve any constructive purpose, other than giving a sense of pleasure to sadistic elements in the population, it must achieve this by discouraging future anti-social activities. To the degree, instead, that it teaches anti-social behavior, it fails. A convincing argument on logical grounds alone can be advanced to justify the punitive approach to the elimination of anti-social behavior. The argument would describe "respectable, law-abiding society" as made up of people who deliberately choose conventional, "law-abiding" behavior over any other because they prefer it, and then cherish the kind of recognition and acceptance they thereby gain from other, conventional, "law-abiding" citizens. It can be granted that some people, however, do not prefer this mode and place no value on the public opinion which a "law-abiding" approach to life might evoke. These people commit crimes, but, punishment could, theoretically, instill in them the fear of behaving anti-socially—the fear of repeated punishment. This reasoning can justify the prison experience. Chances are that most citizens would endorse the wisdom of this argument, even though it is not supported by experience.

The difficulty in making the predictions of the argument come true lies in the readiness with which the offender acquires a *fear of being caught again* rather than *a fear of committing other crimes*. Respectable and responsible people might understand that the best way of avoiding being caught is to not commit a crime again, but they are not the ones who have to learn this. Instead, it is another kind of people caught in the system of law enforcement, people who do not learn the same things, or in the same way.

The student population of the educational environment in the prison constitute a captive population, which, resistant as any group might be to being educated, is, nevertheless, highly impressionable in a certain, peculiar way. The impressionability of this population is like that of a small child's in the sense that the fund of knowledge and skills of its members is so severely limited that a vacuum is thereby created, which, by default, will become filled with whatever manages to creep in. Other, more knowledgeable people, have greater reservoirs of knowledge and skills which serves to screen out much new information as useless or incorrect. Without this means of competition between old and new information, new information tends to get lodged unscreened, unsorted and unjudged except by primitive and simplistic screening devices. Anything which is understandable tends to be believable in the absence of other theories. Any information which helps distinguish the safe from the unsafe tends to be remembered. Above all, negative conclusions (conviction that something is false) are easier to arrive at, requiring fewer clues, than positive conclusions (convictions that something is true).

Thus, learning tends to consist of an expanding list of what to avoid, and a diminishing list of what to do. Typically, this population starts out in adult life with a set of narrow and limited experiences and then progressively restricts activities to even narrower limits as the members advance in age. At age 20, one of these typical youthful offenders might be engaged in drinking, fighting and stealing. At 30, he is drinking and stealing, and at 40, he is only drinking. The popular mythology portrays the life of the offender as one which progresses successively up a ladder of more and more serious crimes. The opposite is much more common, except that with the changes taking place as old behaviors are abandoned, he remains, nevertheless, still a social problem.

The opportunities available in the prison educational environment for the inmate to learn and to try conventional, socially accepted behavior are confronted with insuperable obstacles, and massive contradictions. In the first place, the prison demands that he be a *good* prisoner, and *good* is defined as one who scrupulously obeys all the rules. The rules, in turn, are manifold, constantly changing and generally increasing in number. Invariably, the rules are imposed entirely by someone else, are not only arbitrary in their own right, but their arbitrariness is forcibly emphasized. The prisoner is now confronted with a dilemma almost impossible to resolve. In order to shorten his sentence as much as possible, by being a *good* prisoner, and in order to avoid the extra punishments which result if he fails, he has to learn to behave in a way which, if followed outside the prison, would make him almost totally helpless. The outside requires taking responsibility, using one's own judgment, making one's own decisions. The prison society specifically and massively pro-

hibits this. The longer the stay in prison, the farther removed
the offender is from any skills he might once have had for independent living.

The behavior expected of the prisoner toward others is
dictated by the rules which prescribe his reactions to prison
officials. His behaviors toward other prisoners tend to be looked
upon with suspicion, no matter what they seem to consist of, so
are discouraged by numerous prohibitions. With the guards, the
personnel with whom he is in daily contact, he is expected,
above all, to display a proper attitude. The typical lack of sophistication of guard personnel interprets attitude in terms of what
the prisoner says and the tone of voice used. Thus, a proper
show of respect to the guards is demanded.

On the other hand, almost nothing of substance is provided
the prisoner to command the respect he is expected to show.
Guards characteristically present themselves to prisoners as in-
credibly lazy people, with no discernible skills, who mostly stand
around doing nothing except to give orders. There is, perhaps,
no group of people in the entire American culture who would
find less to admire in this model than the prison population.
Thus, one of the commonest rules broken, and the commonest
cause of extra punishment consists of disrespectful statements
prisoners make toward guards. This apparent super-sensitivity
of guards to verbal abuse reinforces the already deeply entrenched defensiveness of the prisoner himself. Defending his
so-called honor against the verbal insults of his peers has already
been a life-long preoccupation with him, and the prison society
intensifies the preoccupation.

Again, the great impact these kinds of experiences has on
the prisoner—that is, suffering punishment after insulting guards—
is a by-product of the poverty of competing experiences which,
if they had been more plentiful, might have served to diminish
the importance of the experiences in question. What the prisoner
is most likely to learn in these painful experiences is to seek the
kind of power over other people which can extract punishment
of them for their insults, as the guards seem to do.

When the prisoner is brought before higher officials to be

punished for infraction of the rules, he learns another set of behaviors which help him adapt to the prison society. Usually, after first having tried a defiant approach, with painful consequences, he might eventually learn how to make the expected impression. He will learn, then, that a show of contriteness produces better results than defiance, even though the latter approach is the more honest one. Once he has learned how to act with a suitable degree of penitence, he is well on his way to becoming *jail wise,* and thereby getting his first lessons in how to be a good *con man.* If he learns these skills well, he might well succeed then in staying out of prison when he gets out, not at the price of giving up his delinquent life, but by developing better skills in getting away with it.

It is, perhaps, the arbitrariness of the rules and of the punishment meted out that has the greatest educational impact on the youthful offender. Rarely, if ever, are rules justified, explained, or made internally consistent. Instead, they are presented as rules for the sake of rules—rules as an end in themselves—not as rules for the sake of governing the institution. The lesson expected to be learned by the prisoner is that following the rules makes good prisoners, and good prisoners make good citizens. Stupid as the typical prison population is, few are stupid enough to believe this. Instead, what the prisoner learns is that rules are a way to exercise power over others—and the arbitrary exercise of power is a desirable goal to strive for.

Hence, the prisoner hopes and tries to emulate what he sees when he gets power over others—the imposition of arbitrary rules on others' behavior. Typically, then, when he gets out of prison he seeks relationships with people (usually women) over whom he can exercise such power, or he tries to dominate other prisoners while in prison in the same way. Unwittingly, then, he sows the seeds of others' betrayal of him, and others would include wife and children, for instance. Just as he starts out in adolescence as the victim of others' domination against which he will rebel as soon as he can, he will seek to dominate others who will, in turn, rebel against him. The frequency with which prisoners fantasy a utopia in which they have power over others leads them to make relationships with women with this in mind—thus, pimping becomes one of the favorite post-graduate careers which they try to enter.

The absence of due process in the prisoner's set of rights specifically teaches him to expect little from conventional legal systems in the pursuit of his goals. Furthermore, the due process rights he had prior to conviction never seemed to him to have been fair. Many studies of prisoners point out that prisoners characteristically insist on their innocence. These protestations tend to be so unconvincing and superficial, however, that they can be easily penetrated. Instead, what the typical prisoner is more likely to emphasize is not that he was innocent of the crime, but that he knows of many others who were far more guilty, of far more crimes, and they were not convicted. Middle class, conventional citizens are not likely to be acquainted with these kind of people, but the people who inhabit prisons are very well acquainted with them, and are very much impressed with how much crime goes unpunished. They resent as unfair their having been punished on the grounds that the others have not been. In short, these experiences scarcely enhance the prisoner's image of society as a lawful and orderly system.

Clearly, the route by which students learn most from teachers is by imitation. Students, if they learn anything from teachers are most likely to learn what the teacher *does* rather than what the teacher *says*. The principal representative of conventional society which the prisoner is in contact with is the prison guard. He sees the guard as having these characteristics: the guard is totally without any discernible (to the prisoner, at least) occupational skills; he is unbelievably lazy, he has power over others (the prisoners); and he exercises this power through the enforcement of arbitrary rules in an arbitrary manner. With it all, the guard seems to be well paid, well fed (from the prisoner's vantage point), and stands in favorably with society. Converting this lesson into career plans for himself, he can endorse the general outline, for it fits his own irresponsible prejudices. Thus, he hopes for a future when he, too, can live comfortably without working (the way he pictures the guard's job) but by controlling others to do his bidding.

RESPONSIBILITY OF THE PRISON FOR EDUCATION: As defined above, the complete control which the prison exercises over the decisions of the prisoner population imposes a responsibility, and demands an accountability to society. Above all, society is concerned with what the prisoner takes away from his prison experience to his subsequent life outside. The only thing he can take is what he might have learned. Heretofore, it appears that prisons have seen the world outside to which the prisoner is eventually to be discharged as one portrayed in 19th century myths, but not one in actual existence.

The world outside is not a place where adjustment is determined by ability to follow arbitrary rules set by someone else. Instead, it is a very heterogeneous place with multiple problems in which adjustment is determined by mature and independent decision-making, on one's own and with one's own resourcefulness. It is hopeless for the prison to try to convince anyone, prisoners or anyone else, that being in prison is meant by society to be for any other purpose than punishment. Nevertheless, the prison can justifiably detach itself from certain aspects of the punishment inasmuch as it was a court, not the prison, which imposed it.

The social role of the prison in the life of the youthful offender (much more so than in the life of the older offender) is not unlike that of the parent toward the child. In both cases, supposedly mature and socially responsible adults have life-and-death levels of control over the decision-making of impressionable, immature youths who will eventually have to face the problem of adjusting to an adult world on their own. This type and level of control, and the resulting potential for spectacular success or disastrous failure are so critical that very careful balances must be achieved between the good that can be done with the harm that is possible.

A proper philosophy to adopt in guiding day-to-day decisions could be feasibly based on the concept that ultimate outcome of the subject population is more important than immediate results. Thus, adjustment to prison life should not be seen as nearly important as what can be done to improve the level of adjustment to post-prison life. Thus, rewards for honesty, hardwork, cooperation with others and ability to plan ahead should be greater than rewards for pleasing prison personnel, obeying commands or following rules. Similarly, punishment would more properly be meted out for failure to contribute to a wife's support, failure to learn an occupational skill or refusing to make plans for the future. Rewards and punishment can be simply confined to the shortening or lengthening of the prison sentence, as a mechanism for teaching that the one, single motive which is present in all prisoners—the desire to get out soon—can be used to give the prisoner some degree of control over his own life.

These remarks point to one of the most significant things which the prisoner has not learned well before, and which he might learn in prison. The prison experience, through the control it has over the prisoner's life, can become the instrument by which the prisoner learns that he can exercise considerable control over his own life, and that this can be done by the process of assuming responsibility. He learns the opposite in the prison system where "getting out early on good behavior" is achieved by obediently following prison rules. Instead, if he could shorten his stay by voluntarily making his own decisions, his own plans, and using his own time to improve his occupational skills, he will be on the way to learning something more valuable.

A not inconsiderable obstacle to the task of bringing about a change in the present correctional system is the fact that workable improvements are very likely to be looked upon by many citizens, legislators, courts and prison officials as personally distasteful to them. Until now, the system in operation has been designed in accordance with what suits the prejudices of these defenders of the social system instead of being in accordance with what works.

CHAPTER VII

NEW APPROACHES TO SOLVING THE PROBLEM

OBSTACLES TO IMPROVEMENT

THE ENTRENCHED ATTITUDES and vested interests of many powerful people stand in the way of developing a more workable corrections system than now exists. To a very large extent, these influences, which generally demand more and more of what has already been done so unsuccessfully, are founded on essentially no knowledge of what prisons are like or on what kind of people are committed to them. The present situation is reminiscent of Supreme Court Justice Louis Brandeis' warning many years ago. He pointed out that the nation has less to fear from its enemies from without than it has from some of its friends from within—friends in the form of "well-meaning, do-gooder legislators who pass laws on subjects they know nothing about." The structure and operation of the nation's correctional system is founded on sets of laws and a system of management designed mostly to make do-gooders feel righteous and not by a theory or practices designed to bring delinquent behavior under better control. Politicians typically manage to get votes on the grounds of harsh public statements they make on "law and order" issues, and then conspicuously violate the laws themselves with apparent immunity. They readily pass laws to punish wrong-doers but not to detect and apprehend them. They appropriate huge sums of money to build expensive prisons then pitifully small sums to staff them. They demand that delinquents be brought to justice, but fail to expedite the machinery of justice.

In short, no evidence has been discernible to indicate that society has heretofore been interested in supporting a system of law enforcement and corrections which is meant to be more than a monument to certain peoples' righteous indignation. Improvements in the system, in order to really be improvements, will require sweeping changes in the entire social system, and not merely superficial changes in prison design or management. Some of the changes which are in order, and which, conceivably are possible, include the following:

RESPECT FOR A LAWFUL AND ORDERLY SOCIETY: Perhaps no recommendation for improvement will be viewed as pessimistically by experts as the one which requires that Americans adopt nationwide respect for law and order. This has never been a conspicuous attribute of the American culture. Instead, Americans have traditionally regarded themselves as capable of managing their affairs with a minimum of restrictions from social control. The American frontier tradition still dominates prevailing attitudes, even though it is woefully outdated. An adventurous, free-wheeling spirit which liberally interprets the rights of the individual to exploit to his own advantage opportunities to advance himself at the expense of others still dominates much of what happens. The development of the nation into the worldwide power it is, from a handful of venturesome pioneers conquering a wilderness did, indeed, depend upon this kind of spirit. Justified or not at one time, its usefulness has long since disappeared. Instead, the nation has suddenly, in this latter part of the twentieth century, become a complex system of interdependent institutions on which has fallen a major share of the responsibility for running the world. The vast responsibility over the power amassed by ingenious entrepreneurial skills in a laissez faire environment of the past cannot be maintained in the same way it was acquired. Instead, a vast increase in the degree of orderliness of management and consistancy in purpose is called for in order to effectively hold on to the accomplishments which have been made. Failure to do so will produce counterrevolutions which will seize control by other forces which have the great advantage of much greater numbers and nothing to lose.

Other cultures which have spawned the American culture are noteworthy for the greater respect their members demonstrate for law and order. The English come closest to ours, and their people are far and away more imbued with a respect for maintaining the integrity of their own system than ours are. Ours, instead are filled with many forces within which are disruptive of the system itself. The Scandanavian cultures, the Netherlanders and Belgians, the Swiss all support the system they have designed for themselves much better than we Americans do our own. Because they have done so much better than we have, it behooves us to see if there is something to learn from what they have done that we might profit from. Two things they generally have done which are different from us are clearly contributory to the cause of improving respect for lawful and orderly society. In the first place, these cultures have not done as we Americans have in the matter of legislating criminal laws. They have not

UNREPORTED CRIMES

Results of survey of 10,000 households by National Opinion Research Center of the University of Chicago, 1965 to 66.

Showing percent of cases in which a crime was committed that was not reported . . . .

CRIME	% Unreported
Robbery	35%
Aggravated assault	35%
Simple assault	54%
Burglary	42%
Larceny (over $50)	40%
Auto theft	11%
Malicious mischief	62%
Consumer fraud	90%
Other fraud (bad checks)	74%
Sex offenses (not rape)	49%
Family crimes (desertion)	50%

The Challenge of Crime in a Free Society, Report of the President's Commission on Law Enforcement and Administration of Justice, Government Printing Office, 1967.

criminalized as many activities as we have, and thus, have not created as many laws which can be broken. It would seem strikingly obvious that the fewer laws that are broken, the more the respect that can be generated for the laws. On the other hand, it seems evident that when widespread lawbreaking exists, then respect for laws must fall to a low ebb. It is a self-defeating and a self-fulfilling system in that widespread law-breaking tends to foster more of the same, just as extensive law abiding tends to perpetuate itself.

A simple and obvious device which can diminish law-breaking is to reduce the number of laws to be broken. There exists two very large areas in the American system which lend themselves to this approach. In the area, for instance, of the *victimless* crime—that is, the morals offenses—there is vast room for reducing the number of law breakers by the simple expedient of reducing the number of laws. The laws which criminalize alcohol and drug abuse, gambling, and sex offenses are striking examples of measures which seek to stamp out practices which, sound though the idea might be, will never be accomplished by making the practices illegal. Decriminalizing these behaviors does not imply that society should then ignore them, but, rather, that other more workable methods need to be used. In no areas does the preventive solution offer more promise, for instance, but as long as society relies on the legalistic solution, inadequate attention will be paid to the other.

Another large area amenable to reduction in numbers of law-breakers through reduction in laws is in the accelerating field of traffic offenses. Clearly, the various regulations needed for management of automobile traffic are most properly viewed as an intrinsic part of the health and safety system of society rather than the law enforcement system. A comprehensive, new regulatory system needs to be designed to encompass all health and safety problems, with specialists in public health and safety involved in the enforcement of standards. New concepts of inspections, detection of violations, and means of insuring compliance with standards are needed, that are unlikely to ever raise the question of police involvement except in cases of criminal negligence or fraud. This area of social order should be philosophically and functionally related to the responsibilities and accountabilities to public health and safety properly associated with the granting of certain privileges such as the privilege of driving a car, of operating a restaurant, etc. The reward and punishment methodology employed would then properly be based on the granting or withholding of privileges. An effective system of regulation would almost never require the use, for instance, of armed policemen, prisons, court proceedings, etc. Already many precedents have been established in this general area, such as public health, industrial safety and air traffic regulations.

A second way in which some of America's mother cultures have progressed beyond our level of respect for an orderly society is noteworthy. In many countries other than ours, there is seen much less evidence of corruption in public officials, a state which immeasurably improves the likelihood of citizens viewing the official system with respect. Our own political system, instead, views with great tolerance the wrong-doing of officials. Very definitely, those spokesmen and leaders who advocate supporting, rather than changing our present law enforcement and corrections system would do well by starting to clean house at the official level. Radical improvements in the caliber of people holding public office are not likely to occur until new and different types of citizens aspire to these offices. At the present time, the unsavory environment of many corrupt political units effectively screen out the kind of people who might clean them up. A factor not well appreciated by conventional law-abiding citizens is the fact that they, themselves, are not the ones likely to come face to face with official corruption. Instead, it is the people who encounter graft and corruption that are the ones prone to delinquent behavior—the ones who could be harmed most by witnessing this model of official behavior.

A general principle should, but does not, prevail in the matter of passing and repealing criminal laws. This principle would properly state that no law should be allowed to stand on the books unless it can be, and is, enforced effectively. It would be better, as far as respect for law is concerned, to repeal a law than to allow it to exist as an unenforced law. To achieve this level of sophistication would require some responsible and effective means of determining enforcibility. If, for instance, it can be

WHITE COLLAR CRIME

The law is pressing in one direction, and other forces are pressing in the opposite direction. In business, the "rules of the game" often conflict with the legal rules . . . . The Better Business Bureaus and Crime Commissions, composed of business and professional men, attack burglary, robbery and cheap swindles, but overlook the crimes of their own members.

White Collar Criminality, E. G. Sutherland, American Sociological Review, Feb. 1940, p. 3.

shown that 90 percent of all violators of a given criminal law are apprehended and brought to justice, this would be a very desirable level of enforcibility. If, however, only 10 percent of violators are apprehended, then this would be a very unsatisfactory level, too low to warrant having the law. Currently, for instance, the laws prohibiting the possession of illegal drugs are so unenforceable that they generate widespread disrespect, in the same way that the Prohibition laws of the 1920's did.

RE-DIRECT ATTENTION TO THE VICTIM OF CRIME: Except for morals offense, nearly all crimes involve damage to the life or property of some other person. If the attention of law enforcement and correction effort, as well public attitudes, were redirected away from the alleged but dubious damage done to society and toward the real and very apparent damage done to the victim, there could result significant changes in both attitudes and policies which could have far reaching effect. For instance, if this re-direction of attention were to occur, then it would be appropriate that the punishment meted out to the offender be in the form of making restitution to the victim. Thus, much of the antagonism now being generated against society by the offender population because of the latter's difficulty in understanding society's role in the affair will be changed. It would be much simpler for the offender to understand the issues if his punishment were in the form of making restitution to the victim. It is conceivable that the nature of the restitution made could often be something negotiated between offender and victim instead of something processed by the laborious and inefficient court system. In most instances, restitution would take the form of paying monetary damages which might be accomplished in a variety of ways over which both victim and offender would have some degree of control. The importance of this phenomenon is that the process of changing other peoples' behavior requires first that they have confidence in the controllability of their own behavior. That is to say, it is hopeless to expect that other people will change from an old to a new style of behavior unless they possess the concept of this being something they can control. The delinquent population is the one that is least likely to have any confidence in the ability to shape their own lives, for they have never seen themselves significantly as having much to say about the subject.

Under a victim-oriented, instead of society-oriented enforcement system, much more responsible action on the part of the victims of crime is required; but, also, they would have much more to gain. Their gain would be restitution of the damages inflicted on them, and this prospect could do more than the present system to motivate them to participate in the enforcement system. Presently, the typical victim sees little advantage to him, and great potential dangers, in offering his cooperation, or in even reporting the crime. More of the burden of proof would have to be placed on the victim to establish proof that a crime was committed, for instance. The courts might well stand in the position of a guarantor of restitution, meaning that this would be done by the court in the event that the enforcement system fails to apprehend the offender. Thus, the cost of poor enforcement would become more visibly demonstrated, and incentives created to improve the system.

Chances are that a very large share of the criminal cases now processed by courts could become civil cases to be processed by simpler and more efficient administrative machinery. This could work wonders in streamlining the courts' responsibilities so that they could specialize more than they do now with the kind of tasks they were meant to perform. Preservation of the American standard of justice, with its complex due process methods, trial by jury and adversary procedures cannot be done by making it a mass production system. It must be reserved for the relatively rare, rather than commonplace, case which cannot be handled by simpler and prompter methods.

PROFESSIONALIZING THE ENFORCEMENT AND CORRECTIONAL SYSTEM: Most of the progressive leaders within the current system have come to realize that much better levels of professional training, conduct and standards are needed in order to improve the system. In the American tradition, extensive professionalization of the system would probably be accompanied by increasing degrees of specialization. As a result, different police officers would specialize in different phases of enforcement, different prisons would specialize in different kinds of prisoner popula-

---

A PROFIT AND LOSS STATEMENT IN MIDDLE-CLASS CRIME

The Wall Street Journal of Jan. 26, 1973 reported what might well be the record-setting crime, when measured in terms of money stolen. A banker of Cartersville, Georgia, pursued a progressively more profitable embezzling practice from 1951 until he was finally caught, tried and convicted recently. Altogether, he was believed to have stolen $4,611,473 from the bank; but at no time, even after his conviction, was he ever looked upon by his community as anything other than one of its leading citizens. He expressed no regrets, but a sense of relief, over his conviction, and plans to spend his forthcoming prison sentence writing a book on how to detect and prevent such crimes. None of the stolen money was recovered, meaning that the offender can now weigh the profit of over four million dollars against the loss of ten years of his liberty. (His prison sentence was ten years.) Interestingly, and paradoxically (when viewed as a profit and loss issue), three young men were recently sentenced in the same court for robbing another local bank of $13,834, but their sentences were for 16 years each! Theirs was the more conventional way of robbing banks; however, a way which society seems to regard as more reprehensible.

---

tions, different courts would specialize in different kinds of cases, etc. This is already happening in steadily increasing degrees, but without very much evidence of professionalizing the personnel and the institutions. The feasibility of carrying this recommendation forward would be greatly increased if the mass of work to be done could be reduced to a more manageable level. This, in turn, could be accomplished by the other recommendations made which are designed to streamline the system by diverting many of the current responsibilities into more appropriate channels. The federal police have come closest to this goal, and have clearly profited from it by enjoying a much better reputation, and by having done a much better job. However, it, too, is now in the process of having a great many poorly thought out tasks dumped, piecemeal, in its lap—such as the skyjacking problem, for instance.

In order for professionalization of the system to be a great improvement over the present system, it would be necessary that the professionalized personnel accept a much greater degree of responsibility for shaping policy, setting standards, and policing themselves. It is this kind of responsibility which makes a profession truly professional. It is quite evident that present personnel in the system see themselves, and are seen by others, as mere servants in the system. Thus, it is most likely to work out successfully, if personnel from older professions are used as much as possible in order to bring to the new professional field the concepts of professionalism. To a large extent, the federal police accomplished this by selecting lawyers and CPA's for many of their posts, even though their new responsibilities were those of policemen.

NEW VIEW OF THE PRISON'S RESPONSIBILITY: The court, which processes the crime brought to its attention in the person of the offender, sees its responsibility as having come to an end when it imposes the sentence. The prison, on the other hand, must regard its responsibility as something which begins with the imposition of the sentence. In order for the prison to make any headway in bringing about a favorable change in the prisoner while he is serving his sentence, some minimal degree of cooperation must be elicited. Eliciting cooperation from one whom the institution is charged with punishing presents nearly insurmountable obstacles. Some kind of new and philosophically different approach to the prison's responsibility must be devised in order to develop the basis for the cooperation needed between institution and inmate. A simple solution, and one which could be understandable to the limited intelligence of the prison population, is feasible.

The standard hue and cry from so-called, well-meaning, but poorly informed, liberally-minded reformers demands that prisons fulfill a *rehabilitation* role. Although this makes sense, and should not be disparaged, it more often than not misses the point. *Rehabilitation* is not some magical innovation, but is nothing more nor less than *education*. (The French refer to rehabilitation as re-education.) As indicated above, education always takes place in every prison, which is saying the same thing as saying that all prisoners get *rehabilitation*. However, education (or rehabilitation) can be either good or bad. What is scarce in prisons is not *education,* but enough of *good education* to neutralize and nullify or diminish the effects of the *bad education* that the prisoner will get just because he is in prison with a lot of other people like himself.

A feasible way by which the prison administration can make inroads into the prisoners' resistance to cooperation is through adopting a new approach to the way it pictures its punitive role to the prisoner, and to itself. In the first place, the prison administration will lose credibility with the prisoners if it claims that its role is not a punitive one. The punitive role might as well be admitted freely in order to start off on a level of understanding with the prisoners. The prison administration can then portray its responsibility in this punitive task as being that of making the punishment as brief as possible. The prisoner would then be given a very straightforward and concrete list of things both he and the prison can do to either prolong or shorten the sentence. In general, what the prison could do would be in the form of offering the prisoners opportunities for taking responsibility, and what the prisoners could do (or not do) would be to accept these opportunities. The more responsibility the prisoner accepts, the shorter his sentence, and vice versa; the less responsibility he accepts, the longer the sentence. However, the limit

CHANGE VERSUS STATUS QUO IN CHOICE OF OFFENSE

In the study reported in this book, the first offense of each case was compared with the last one. Those showing change and those not showing change in choice of offense is thus illustrated.

FIRST OFFENSE	LAST OFFENSE	% OF POPULATION
	(STATUS QUO CASES)	
Theft	(same)	65%
Assault	"	4%
Disorderly conduct	"	4%
Murder	"	1%
	Total	74%
	(CHANGE IN OFFENSE)	
Assault	Theft	9%
Disorderly conduct	Assault	5%
Disorderly conduct	Theft	3%
Forgery	"	1.3%
Narcotics	"	1.3%
Rape	Assault	1%
Rape	Theft	1%
(None)	Rape	1%
Narcotics	Disorderly conduct	0.4%
Murder	Assault	0.4%
Rape	Disorderly conduct	0.4%
Traffic	Theft	0.4%
	Total	24.2%

to his stay would be the one set by the court as the maximum sentence. The minimum length would be the time required to demonstrate convincing degrees of having accepted major responsibilities.

For instance, a situation in which a prisoner would be able to demonstrate willingness and ability to accept major amounts of responsibility would be one which closely simulates a responsible life outside the prison. He might, for example, hold down a full-time skilled job, at standard wages. From his wages he would pay the prison for his room and board and contribute to the support of his family at home. In his spare time, he could be advancing his education. At the other extreme, there should be permitted the option for the prisoner who chooses to do nothing useful while in prison, and thereby serves a maximum sentence, as a glaring example to all of the fruits of non-productivity. A simple, arithmetical way of calculating how the prisoners' choices of activity could effect his length of stay would be in order as a way to maximize the prisoners' capacity to understand the new system. Each day of his prison life could be rated as a productive or a non-productive day, and degrees of productivity could range from one-half to two. For every productive unit he earned, there would be subtracted an equal number of days from his maximum sentence. Half units would be in order because it could often happen that a half-day's work or similar activity, rather than a full-day's, would apply to particular days. On the other hand, each day would have the equivalent of two eight hour periods to expend, and if both were spent productively (one in a full-time job, the other in education, for instance), he could earn two units. Thus, the range of lengths of stay could vary from about one third to the maximum sentence.

In order for such a system to be effective, the prison would have to take responsibility for providing a full range of responsible activities for each prisoner to engage in. In some instances, a prisoner would have to first learn a skill before he could assume a responsible job. However, if a prison could succeed in adopting such a system, it would thereby provide a basis for the administration to establish a business-like level of cooperation with each prisoner devoid of the necessity of trying to win cooperation on more nebulous grounds.

ALTERNATIVES TO PRISON: For the major bulk of the youthful offender population now inhabiting prisons and other similar institutions, it is evident that something important is so defective with their environment that some sort of placement elsewhere is called for. It is most often the absence of other alternatives which results in this group being sent to prison rather than prison being a prime choice. Nevertheless, of all people who get sent to prison, this is the group which can be harmed the most, yet perhaps the one which could be helped the most if something better were available. What is clearly needed for this group is a new kind of experience which would help them grow into responsible adults by association with other people who could

CRIME IN NEW YORK AND LONDON

The New York Times reported on March 12, 1973, the incidence of crime in New York City as compared with that of London for the year 1972. The two cities are comparable in size, but show a marked difference in incidence of reported crime.

OFFENSE	LONDON	NEW YORK
Murder	113	1,691
Rape	135	3,271
Robbery	3,167	78,202
Assault	7,861	37,130

show them a reasonable model of responsibility. The prison, unfortunately, offers the opposite kind of influence. It is often quite true that removal from their previous homes and community environment is highly in order, but no improvements can be predicted unless the new environment is a better one. Perhaps no existing institutionalized environment could serve the purpose better than the military life. Conceivably, if the typical youthful offender could be placed in a military unit which voluntarily was prepared to accept him, and if he was the only offender among a group of other young men with conventional backgrounds and standards, he could find the leadership and influence he needs to mature successfully. Experience shows that this, indeed, often happens, though seldom in a deliberate and calculated way. The peacetime military services might well take on this responsibility officially in the future. If this were to happen, many desirable results could be expected. In the first place, the delinquent would be removed from the home and community where he had gotten into trouble, and which, presumably was unsuited for him, and vice versa. Secondly, society could view the placement with considerable composure since the delinquent would thereby fall under the scrutiny and guidance of society's representatives in the armed forces. Lastly, the youth could get the opportunity he never had before of starting off a new life with associates that could be an asset instead of a liability to him, while being exposed to the chance of learning adult skills.

For the offender already tried and convicted, other alternatives to prison have alrealy been tried with varying degrees of success. The extended use of probation as an alternative, for instance, is not likely to be an improvement unless substantial professional guidance is given the offender during the probation period. Currently, the management of the offender during probation rests in the hands of probation officers which are often poorly trained, and if not, are too often overloaded with work. Perhaps most important of all is the necessity of building into the probation system (in addition to qualitative and quantitative adequacy of manpower) a systematic long-term follow-up procedure which feeds useful information about outcomes back into the input stage. At the present time, there is inadequate long-range evaluation of methods, irrelevant training of personnel, and defective criteria for rendering service. Too often, for instance, the most promising cases are ignored on the grounds that they need the least help and manpower is wasted on the others who do not profit from the help given. A *triage* system is needed which more selectively screens into the probationary process those who both need help and are likely to profit from help, and screens out of the process those who do not need help and those who will not profit. Only diligent and objective long-term follow-up studies will develop the necessary data.

Other, more novel, alternatives have also been used recently, and sometimes with great success in reducing prison populations. Half-way houses are examples. The danger in all novel experiments is that they tend to get themselves loudly promoted by non-objective enthusiasts and then the experiment backfires when others try the same experiment, but get poor results. This tendency to mount fashionable bandwagons needs to be stringently curbed, to be supplanted by carefully controlled, objective experiments devoid of promotional tactics. A tendency will be discovered for almost any new experiment to seem to work, due to the well known, but poorly appreciated "Hawthorne effect." This effect refers to the tendency of groups of impressionistic people to be positively influenced by any change in the approach used. It is not unlike the "placebo effect" of medicine. Appreciating the likelihood of the new seeming to work better than the old can be deliberately exploited, and need not be disparaged. The new tends to breed a certain optimism and enthusiasm among the personnel employing it, which can be contagious to the recipients of service, and this attitude can, indeed, produce positive results. The same technique is not so likely to work later for someone else, however, for the second experiment is more likely to be conducted with a certain cynicism, which has poor motivating effects.

PREVENTION—NEW LEADERSHIP: For the bulk of the delinquent population described before as the "passive army of followers," it would make sense for social institutions to seek means of correcting the deficiency of masculine leadership in these youths' lives. The efforts that have been made to correct this problem have generally started too late, that is, at the time when the youths are dropping out of high school. In order to have an impact, a start needs to be made long enough ahead of this time to forestall the vicious history of failures, of which school drop-out is only a late example. Masculine leadership is most acutely needed as an adolescent passes through puberty and thus begins to wean himself from mother's influence. In school terms, this would mean during the junior high school years, occurring about the ages of 13 to 15. At the present time, school systems are notably lacking in male teachers at this level because male teachers tend to acquire and to qualify for what schools label as the higher career route of "secondary education," meaning high school. For the population at issue, however, highly trained pedagogues may not be nearly as important as men with simpler ambitions who are prepared to dedicate themselves to offering leadership for a lot of essentially fatherless boys, and probably in the least attractive schools. If there is any logical place in the educational system for a large physical education program, it would be at this level. If, for instance, less demand were made on these boys for academic achievement and more ways sought to keep them interested in school, perhaps much could be accomplished. Doing this might require very untraditional ways of using school resources because what would need to be provided the adolescents in question would be attributes provided by most homes, but lacking in the homes of these boys. The objective would be to provide the masculine leadership needed to provide a male adult model for the boys of responsible, satisfying living.

Other resources in the community might also be mobilized to supply similar kinds of leadership in competition with the destructive leadership of the street gang. Doing this would probably require the enlistment of the entire gang in new ventures which would have to be of enough interest to the members to insure their participation, but pointed toward more constructive ends. A ready arena in which to launch such a program would be one which would be centered on those few activities in which these boys can be interested, such as sports and automobiles. It would be important that the leaders provided be not too far removed culturally from the boys, for too much cultural distance could sabotage the plan.

RE-ORIENTATION OF THE OCCUPATION ENTRY SYSTEM: The present century has been characterized by a type of development which serves as an obstacle to employment to many people, but which society is officially unaware of as an obstacle. The increasing institutionalization of work in this century has added a progressively increasing list of rigid procedures which have to be surmounted before an individual can be employed. At the beginning of the century, in contrast, an inexperienced youth could much more easily enter the system, with few obstacles to surmount. Today, however, the child labor and workmen's compensation laws prohibit a young man from getting any work experience until he first passes some minimum age. He has to enroll with Social Security before he can even apply for a job. When he applies, he almost certainly will have to be literate enough to fill out some sort of application form—a familiar enough device with the experienced portion of the population, but incomprehensible to the others. Before any employer will hire him, he first has to be worth the minimum wage, whatever that might be, and the chances of this being the case in view of his complete lack of experience is slim, indeed. In order to hold on to a job, he must be imbued with an uncharacteristic, middle class preoccupation with keeping appointments—that is, getting to work on time, not to mention that he would also have to manage some sort of transportation which might also be non-existent.

On the job, he must be willing and able to accept what will surely seem like humiliating domination from a supervisor. Above all, he must be prepared to take such a long-term view of his life that he would be willing to cope with all kinds of unfamiliar annoyances in order to rise to a position he desires—and this long-term view is probably something he never even heard of, let alone mastered.

Conventional middle and working class youths who have had the benefit of a working father to serve as a model will have become prepared for the plunge into the occupational world, and will circumvent these manifold obstacles. The kind of youth who ends up repeatedly in trouble with the police is not likely to have had any experience or guidance to help him. When he drops out of school at age 16, he has an idea that freedom and pleasure lie ahead through the affluence he will acquire through work. However, when he confronts the task of getting his first job, he is disillusioned to find that he is worth nothing to any employer, and the obstacles he has to overcome to get into a job are beyond his capacity to cope. It is no wonder, then, that he never gets anywhere occupationally . . . for he never gets a start.

There is needed newly designed entry points and methods into the occupational world that inexperienced youth can better cope with. A more gradual transition from inexperienced adolescence to skilled adult can make the transition more feasible. Above all, there is need for a useful economic role for the youth between the ages of 16 and 18 who has dropped out of school, but is not suited for commercial or industrial employment yet, but in this role, he could prepare for the adult world of work. It is not likely that this need will be filled by any program which is called, or which looks like education, for this kind of youth is most unreceptive to this approach—in spite of the fact that this might be exactly what he needs most. Again, the kind of experiences other youths get in their homes and by virtue of their staying in the school system are denied the delinquent-prone group, and, therefore, some sort of substitute needs to be provided. A sort of *junior apprenticeship* to prepare for the adult occupational world is required. This might be provided by the military services, particularly in peacetime, not in the form of a standard enlistment, but in a modified form, characterized by much less of a commitment required of the applicant. In connection with this recommendation, it would be timely for the military services to devise new social roles for themselves which are broader than the traditional defense role, and more adapted to a peacetime kind of operation.

NEW PROGRAMS FOR THE MULTI-PROBLEM FAMILY: The multi-problem family that produces the delinquent youth should become the proper target of attention for long-range prevention programs. An ideal solution might be posed as an objective to work toward. It would seem obvious that contemporary society must accept the fact that the breeding and rearing of children constitutes a major responsibility for which only qualified people should aspire. Unfortunately, the opposite is the case—that is, the most qualified people approach the task most cautiously and least frequently while the least qualified approach it carelessly and most frequently. Extensive family planning programs, liberalized abortion procedures and more streamlined systems for channeling unwanted children into adopted homes could help some. However, the target population in question is apt to be least closely in touch with public education programs, least likely to cooperate with help programs and least aware of the problems they generate by having children born and raised in disruptive homes. Coercive power available to courts in keeping with their custodianship of the rights of children is seldom used to effect changes, but might well be more extensively used. The families in question often come to the attention of social institutions when it is evident that they are doing an inadequate job of caring for their children. At these times, courts might step in and force the family to give up the children for others to raise. The occasions that give substantial clues to the situation in question are those when children of these families are seen in hospitals and clinics as *battered* children, when learning and behavior problems turn up in school and when parents get into trouble with the law. Although it seems, at present, unlikely that strong coercive approaches will be extensively employed in the future to accomplish these ends, it is conceivable that much good can be done by seeking voluntary cooperation to do the same thing. At least, a widespread public education program is in order, one calculated to impress all prospective parents with the terrible responsibility of having children. Of course, this plan could only work if there were also plenty of very responsible families prepared to adopt the children given up by the problem families in question. The current sharp decline in birth rates might increase the number of such families willing to accept an assignment.

Another procedure which could yield desirable effects, but which would probably sound very unsavory to our American tradition, might be mentioned. Various kinds of bargains could be used to negotiate with problem parents certain desired privileges in exchange for accepting voluntary sterilization. This could be a bargaining point for probation or parole for convicted offenders, for instance. Offhand, such a program would sound much like the discredited Eugenics Movement of the 1920's. Therefore, it would not be likely to receive much acclaim. Nevertheless, it should be considered as one of the alternatives open and worth considering. Ultimately, stringent measures designed to limit the size of problem families could greatly improve the chances of these families making a go of it in their own lives, and this fact could justify what might otherwise seem like very un-American methods. On the other hand, it is conceivable that a relatively brief experiment with an extensive program of this sort might prove so effective in reducing delinquency that it could be safely terminated after a while. It has been said, with some justification, that qualifications for having children should, at least, be as strict as qualifying for a mortgage. An interesting parallel between these remarks and mortgaging practices can be cited. It has been reported that when a family applies for a mortgage from certain lending institutions, an unusual type of bargaining sometimes takes place. This happens in cases where the ability of the family to meet mortgage payments is contingent on both husband and wife earning income from full-time jobs. Some banks will agree to lend the money only if the parents submit to sterilization, on the grounds that an unplanned pregnancy could interfere with ability to pay.

RE-ALIGNMENT OF DIVISION OF RESPONSIBILITIES: At the present time, the entire nation's enforcement system is characterized by vast differences in nearly every variable which effects enforcement adequacy. There exists, in the first place, three distinct levels of jurisdiction—the local, state and federal—all of which are represented at each locality. Each has distinct differences in qualifications, adequacy versus shortage in numbers, ranges of salary and degrees of dedication versus degrees of corruption. Between local and between state units there also exists extensive differences in the variables which determine effectiveness. On the one hand, this disparity and non-uniformity can be looked upon tolerantly on the grounds that the differences are related to other, socio-economic factors which are inevitable. However, the differences also serve self-defeating ends which would be comparable to an army in combat having different units with widely varying degrees of strength versus weakness. The clever enemy is most apt to exploit the weak links in the chain, thus rendering the stronger ones ineffective. Similarly, the delinquent world keeps track of the weak links in the enforcement system and then takes advantage of them. This other world, one which the conventional middle class citizen is unaware of, knows where it is safest to conduct gambling operations, where one is least likely to be arrested for fencing stolen cars, where the police can be bribed, etc. In other words, the current piecemeal system characterized by wide differences in enforcement competency inevitably result in weak links which can be, and extensively are, exploited by those who are in touch with the appropriate information. Unfortunately, for the sake of society's orderly governance, the wrong people possess this information, and the others do not. Organized crime exists solely because of its ability to exploit these differences.

A division of responsibility needs to be established nationwide which seeks to diminish the weak points in the system, by providing greater degrees of uniformity in adequacy of enforcement. Local police and police courts (magistrate's courts), whether in a sparsely populated rural county or a large metropolis should most appropriately, perhaps, concentrate on the task of demonstrating a "police presence." Too much of their attention needs to be paid to routine, essentially non-threatening issues of human behavior to result in effective crime control in the impacted areas. The criminal laws, except for the minor ones, would most appropriately be the ultimate responsibility of the state police and branches of state courts. In order to make the state police become oriented exclusively to this task, however, it would be expedient to free them of routine civil cases and traffic problems, which could be turned over to local jurisdictions. Thus, a statewide enforcement system could be devoted to a relatively narrow spectrum of offenses, the ones which require the greatest investigative skills and facilities, but which would not be large in numbers. This kind of division of responsibility could then justify a sharp up-grading of qualifications and rewards for state police, state prosecutors and judges, since the volume of work would be small, but difficult, In other words, this kind of division of responsibility could justify the immediate professionalization of this level of the enforcement system. State universities might very appropriately lead the way in bringing this change about.

If the various state police and courts systems became up-graded to a fairly uniform level of professional competence, it would also make sense to re-appraise the proper role of the federal police. Too much pressure now is applied to shift more and more enforcement responsibility on the FBI because of the poor reputations previously earned at local and state police levels. The professionalization of the state police-court systems could relieve this pressure, and leave the FBI solely concerned with its large volume of civil cases and those complex issues concerning international problems.

Another pressing re-division of responsibility is in order. The police, courts, and prisons are primarily charged with a certain kind of responsibility which is fundamentally and philosophically in conflict with another one which they are sometimes asked to assume. The responsibility for investigating crime, arresting offenders, proving them guilty and confining them to prison requires a type of person and a policy of operation which is contradictory to the rehabilitative role asked of them. Probation and parole, educational and rehabilitation programs in prison, public education and crime preventive programs are of an entirely different order. These tasks require a very different type of person, and a very different philosophy of operation; they should, therefore, not be assigned to the same system. It would seem most appropriate for state departments of education, instead, to assume responsibility for these rehabilitative roles, in much the same way that they have entered, for instance, into vocational rehabilitation for the handicapped. Similarly, the health and safety agencies of the state should properly be assigned the responsibilities for coping with the problems of alcohol and drug abuse.

An important issue rarely discussed is also involved in the above suggestions. As previously reported at length, the world of delinquency survives and flourishes in society to a large extent because of the neglect accorded it and the ignorance of its nature on the part of conventional members of society. The police and prisons alone are in contact with this world; but they, too, are essentially outside the conventional social world. It is timely to bring other portions of society into contact with delinquency in order to maximize the prospects of improving the current level of sophistication. Only through improvements in the state of knowledge by the general public will the needed changes in laws and social attitudes be feasible.

APPENDIX

HISTORICAL LANDMARKS IN THE FIELD OF CORRECTIONS

Date   Event

1166 King Henry II, in England, formalized court procedures in much the same form they remain today. Grand and petit juries were defined, the sheriff was recognized as an officer of the law, and the construction of jails was authorized. "Offenses against the king's peace" provided for the first classification of offenses: arson, robbery, murder, counterfeiting, crimes of violence.

1215 King John was forced by his barons to issue the *Magna Carta,* which established the concept of an Englishman's civil rights through curtailment of the power of the government over the governed. These concepts provided a basic philosophy for the American Revolution.

1557 The first English workhouse established, known as *Bridewell* (later workhouses in England were then called bridewells).

1596 A workhouse was established at Amsterdam.

1717 America was designated a penal colony by the British Parliament. By 1776 about 100,000 prisoners had been shipped here. This history had much to do with the keen interest by the citizens of the U.S. in the inclusion of a Bill of Rights in the Constitution.

1773 The first American prison was established in Connecticut. An abandoned mineshaft was used to house prisoners and conditions were said to be extremely severe. Other colonies followed this precedent.

1774 The first prison riot in the U.S. occurred, at the first prison.

1777 *The State of the Prisons* was published in England by John Howard. This was the first effort to provide a rationale for the humane treatment of prisoners.

Date   Event

1787   *The Philadelphia Society for Alleviating the Miseries of the Public Prisons* was organized by the Quakers, and included both Benjamin Franklin and Benjamin Rush. That this move was influenced by John Howard's book was evident in the fact that Rush invited Howard (unsuccessfully) to the U.S. just before the latter's death.

1790   The first penitentiary established in Philadelphia, by the above mentioned society. Male and female prisoners were separated, liquor was forbidden, solitary confinement was the rule (to prevent "moral contamination"), and religious instruction was given.

1815   New York State established the first state prison at Auburn. Conditions were much harsher than those in the Philadelphia penitentiary.

1825   A private juvenile institution for delinquents was established in New York.

1829   The first organized, city police system ("Scotland Yard") was established in London following large scale riots. The move was soon followed in the large cities of the U.S.

1847   Public institutions for juvenile offenders were established in New York and Massachusetts.

1867   Michigan passed the first law setting up a parole system. Zebulon Brockway, a prison superintendent, was the leader in this. Other states soon followed the precedent.

1878   Massachusetts became the first state to provide for probation, or suspended sentences (under supervision of the courts).

1899   The first juvenile court was established in Illinois.

1908   The *Federal Bureau of Investigation* was established.

1926   The *Chicago Area Project* was launched by the Institute of Juvenile Research, to study delinquency, in Chicago.

1928   New Jersey first adopted a system for classifying prisoners.

1929   The *Wickersham Commission,* appointed by President Hoover, was the first high-level investigation set up to study law enforcement issues. It was intended to deal chiefly with enforcement of the liquor laws under Pro-

Date   Event

hibition, but the Report produced (1931) was much more comprehensive.

1939- Publication of the Attorney General's *Survey of Release*
1940   *Procedures.* The survey was a WPA project which took place during the early "New Deal" days.

1945   The *New York State Youth Commission* was established to study delinquency in the state.

1947   The *New York City Youth Board* was established to study delinquency in the city.

1950- Publication of the Kefauver *Committee to Investigate*
1951   *Organized Crime.* The investigations preceding the publication were noteworthy for the public attention they received (televised hearings).

1965   Congress passed the *Correctional Rehabilitation Study Act,* to be administered by the Dept. of H.E.W.

1966   Report of the *President's Commission on Law Enforcement and the Administration of Justice.*

INDEX

165